D0886278

LANGUAGES FOR SPECIFIC PURPOSES
PROGRAM DESIGN AND EVALUATION

Ronald Mackay
and
Joe Darwin Palmer
EDITORS

Newbury House Publishers, Inc. / Rowley / Massachusetts / 01969
ROWLEY • LONDON • TOKYO
1981

Library of Congress Cataloging in Publication Data
Main entry under title:

Languages for specific purposes.

Bibliography: p.
Includes index.
1. Languages, Modern--Study and teaching.   2. Lan-
guage planning.   3. Educational accountability.
I. Mackay, Ronald.   II. Palmer, Joe Darwin, 1934-
PB36.L344   407   80-27872
ISBN 0-88377-184-5

NEWBURY HOUSE PUBLISHERS, INC.

Language Science
Language Teaching
Language Learning

ROWLEY, MASSACHUSETTS 01969
ROWLEY ● LONDON ● TOKYO

First printing: April 1981
Printed in the U.S.A.   5   4   3   2   1

Contributors

Lyle F. Bachman, Ph.D., English, Indiana University, is an Assistant Professor in the Division of English as a Second Language, University of Illinois at Urbana-Champaign. His current research interests include the development and construct validation of language proficiency tests, the assessment of language skills needs of foreign students in English-medium universities, language program evaluation, and ESP materials development.

Maryse Bosquet is currently a professor at l'Universite du Quebec and consultant on the design and evaluation of second language programs for several projects in Northern Quebec. She has just completed a teachers' handbook based on the experience she has gained as an elementary and secondary school teacher of French and English, and as a curriculum adviser for the Verdun Catholic School Commission. From 1978 to 1979 she was responsible for the design, implementation, and evaluation of the language maintenance programs (Greek, Italian, and Portuguese) offered by the Ministry of Education of Québec and since 1978 has taught courses at l'Université du Québec in Montreal and at Concordia University.

Bruce L. Derwing, currently Professor of Linguistics at the University of Alberta, Edmonton, was engaged, with Noel Schutz, in a major EST project at the National Central University, Taiwan. Among his many publications is the widely known *Transformational Grammar as a Theory of Language Acquisition,* 1973.

Ronald Mackay received formal training in applied linguistics at the University of Edinburgh and has gained practical experience in most aspects of the field while working and visiting in Scotland, England, Sweden, Denmark, Romania, Bulgaria, Czechoslovakia, Poland, Spain, Morocco, Israel, Singapore, Mexico, the United States, and Canada. Mackay's interests are reflected in his publications in the areas of special purpose language teaching, curriculum design and evaluation, second language reading, and teacher training. He is currently Associate Professor of Applied Linguistics at Concordia University where he also holds the post of Director of ESL Credit and ESL Proficiency Testing.

Joe Darwin Palmer teaches applied linguistics in the Centre for Teaching English as a Second Language, Concordia University, Sir George Williams Campus, in Montreal. He has taught in New York, Michigan, Somalia, Siam, Egypt, Greece, Senegal, and Mexico. He did his graduate work under Albert Marckwardt, Kenneth Pike, James Downer, and Warner Rice.

Martin Keith Phillips is currently Assistant Director of the English Language Centre of King Abdulaziz University, Jeddah, Saudi Arabia. He has more than ten years' experience in EFL, for over half of which he has been involved in the design and implementation of ESL programmes. He has worked in several Middle Eastern locations, including Tabriz, Iran, where he helped develop the "Nucleus: English for Science" materials, as well as assignments in the U.K. He is author of a variety of ESL language materials for areas as diverse as Agriculture, Mathematics, Industry, and Astronomy and has published several papers on ESP methodology. His principal research interest is in the field of ESP syllabus design and methodology and he is particularly interested in the practical aspects of implementing LSP projects.

Noel W. Schutz has been a Program Director for English Language Services and the American Language Academy. While Program Director of the ALA in Tampa, Florida, he co-authored, with Bruce Derwing, the volume, *Essentials of Aviation Mechanics.*

Gregory J. Strick, until recently, was an Assistant Professor of English as a Second Language and Director of the Arya Mehr Project in Iran for the University of Illinois at Urbana-Champaign. He obtained his Ph.D. in

Sociolinguistics at Georgetown University in 1977. He has taught ESL/EFL, trained teachers, and developed programs since 1968 in the United States and the Middle East. His main areas of interest, which include language acquisition, semantic development, research methodology, program design and development, and English for Special Purposes are reflected in his research.

Acknowledgments

The Editors would like to thank the contributors for their original invited contributions which make up Chapters 1, 2, 3, 5, 6, and 7 of this volume. Chapter 4 was originally presented at the Vth AILA Congress held in Montreal in August 1978. It will appear in the proceedings of that congress and is published here in a modified form with the permission of the Canadian organizing committee.

In addition, we gratefully acknowledge the assistance of Concordia University in the preparation of the manuscript version of this book.

Contents

1

LSP Curriculum Development—
From Policy to Practice

Ronald Mackay
Concordia University
Montreal, Quebec

Maryse Bosquet
l'Université du Québec
à Hull

Decision-making in the field of second language teaching takes place on many different levels. It involves individuals whose concerns, functions, and responsibilities, while related to the program and its impact upon the learner and the community in which it is to be implemented, are not identical or even co-extensive. Involved at one point or another are politicians, educators, funding bodies, curriculum planners, materials writers, teacher-trainers, school principals, teachers, evaluators, and researchers, each of whom may be responsible for the planning, modification, or outcome of one or more of the various stages involved in the total language-teaching operation. The entire process has been described by Pit Corder (1973) as a hierarchy of planning functions—all of which, to a greater or lesser extent, are informed by input from applied linguistics. (See Table 1.1.) Although it is uncommon that any

Table 1.1 Hierarchy of planning functions in the total language-teaching operation (Corder, 1973:13)

Level 1	Political	Government	Whether, what language, whom to teach
Level 2	Linguistic Sociolinguistic	Applied linguist	What, when, how much to teach
Level 3	Psycholinguistic	Classroom teacher	How to teach

individual applied linguist would be involved at every level of the planning stages or the decision-making processes associated with an LSP program, it is essential that he or she see the operation in its entirety, for several reasons. The first is that the field of applied linguistics is growing upon an increasingly firm knowledge base supplied by researchers carrying out investigations in a wide variety of areas within what has come to be called the language sciences. These areas of research include studies of language use and language varieties, investigations into ways in which differing learning styles can best be catered to, cognitive and affective factors affecting second language-learning, different roles of formal and informal instruction in acquiring skill in using language, and relationships holding between the development and transfer of language skills, among others. As the knowledge base increases, it is likely that individual applied linguists will be called upon to provide input at a greater number of planning phases and to participate in increasingly extensive decision-making. The second reason is that the better the applied linguist understands the total operation, the greater is the likelihood that his or her contributions will be optimally beneficial. And third, the reduction of the total LSP operation to its characteristic stages can provide the applied linguist with a clearer understanding of them, and, as a result, some indication as to how to manage them most effectively.

It is a characteristic of the real world that constraints operate at every stage, so the better the overall operation is understood by those involved the more likely it will be that the nature of the constraints will be appreciated and seen in perspective. As a result, constraints will be dealt with in such a way as to exercise the least deleterious effect on the final success of the program.

The schema presented in Table 1.2 is an attempt to reduce the ESP curriculum-development operation to its essential stages and to focus in some detail on the phases involved in the program development stage.

PRE-PROGRAM-DEVELOPMENT STAGE

This is a stage of educational decision-making or policy formulation usually accomplished by the administrative body in authority. It might be at the level of a Ministry of Education of an entire country or province. For example, the Polish Ministry of Education may decree that scientific or technical English will be obligatorily taught in all educational and research institutions beyond the B.A. level, the goals being to facilitate the students' reading of specialist literature in their fields of study or research. On the other hand, the commitment to establishing a

Table 1.2   Hierarchy of stages and phases involved in the total curriculum development operation

---

A.   PRE-PROGRAM DEVELOPMENT STAGE
This is typically a stage of educational decision-making in which a policy of educational goals is determined and an interest in and commitment to remedying or changing a situation is expressed in the form of a *rationale.* It can include a *dissemination phase* to enlighten all interested parties and to invite their reactions.

B.   PROGRAM DEVELOPMENT STAGE
This stage can be broken up into a number of phases, some of which may be carried out concurrently. Others may depend upon a strict sequence being observed.

Basic Information-Gathering Phase

Focus on Purpose

Point of departure: Questionnaires, interviews, observations, and checklists

Provide   Information about student needs

From which are identified   Special purposes in terms of the operational skills to be developed in the learner,

Goal-Specification Phase

And   Translation of student needs into pedagogically attainable objectives;

Production Phase

Focus on Language and Language Use

On the basis of which are selected   Texts (oral and/or written)

Which provide   Descriptions of some or all of the language deemed necessary

Focus on Teaching, Learning, and Testing

From which are selected and sequenced   Teaching points

On the basis of which   Teaching materials and testing instruments are developed
(continued on page 4)

Table 1.2 (continued)

And	Appropriate methodological procedures are devised
Teacher-Training Phase	*Focus on Teacher-Training*
And	Appropriate teacher-training is undertaken.
Trial Phase	*Focus on Formative Evaluation*
Then	Materials are taught under observed conditions to determine their day-to-day effectiveness and modified in the light of feedback
And	The congruence between the goals set and student performance is determined. Materials and methodological procedures are revised in the light of this information. Unforeseen effects of the program are recorded.

C. PROGRAM MAINTENANCE AND QUALITY CONTROL STAGE

This stage is concerned with monitoring the quality of the instruction and appropriateness of the goals set, the teacher training, and the testing procedures. It is perhaps a less exciting and creative stage than the previous two, but nonetheless important if the value of the time, effort, and money expended up to this point is to be realized effectively.

Special Purpose Language-teaching program may be made by an institution such as a college of engineering, an (English or American) Language Institute, or a technical school.

Whatever the administrative level at which this decision is made or this policy formulated, the context out of which it arises is usually either a dissatisfaction with the status quo or an awareness of the emergence of a new need. For example, the joint decision of the Colombian and British governments and the Mexican and British governments to fund the development of Special Purpose English Language-teaching programs at undergraduate level in the universities of Colombia and Mexico arose out of the observation that the general language programs currently in operation were not training students to the level of proficiency in English deemed necessary for use as an auxiliary skill to facilitate their academic studies. Or, for example, the ESP program mounted in the University of Kuala Lumpur, Malaysia, was seen by the Ministry of Education as an instrument to ensure adequate English reading standards by university students who had received most or all of their elementary and secondary education in the vernacular since the introduction of the national language, Bahasa Malaysia, as the medium of education in the public school system. Also, the mounting of occupational and professional French language courses by educational institutions in Quebec arose from the need for English-speaking employees to be able to work in the French language as decreed by the Quebec government.

The outcome of the pre-curriculum development stage of decision-making in the total language-teaching operation is a formal commitment of material (including financial and human resources) and moral support for the implementation of the policy deemed necessary to ensure that the requirements of the situation are met.

The policy or rationale may be phrased in the most general of terms, such as "Steps will be taken to ensure that all students reach a level of proficiency in English that will permit them to read textbooks in their field of study," or "All employees on the oil rig will be trained to perform their jobs in English."

Once the rationale for the program has been expressed and the funds committed, it is highly advantageous to include a phase in which the intention to develop the program is diffused widely. It should be made known to all those centrally, and even peripherally, involved--administrators, employers, teachers, teacher-training institutions, students, employees, and even publishers of didactic materials. The purpose of this dissemination phase is to make all those who might be affected by the policy aware of the changing circumstances and new intentions, and to encourage comments, queries, suggestions, or criticism by as broad a range of interested parties as possible. Of course, this initial open-door approach does not exclude the likelihood of directly inviting the reactions of certain individuals or groups of individuals at this point and at later stages. It simply ensures that the widest possible input is provided for at the outset.

A pause for general reaction prior to taking any program development steps has frequently brought to light useful information which the planners were previously unaware of. For example, dissemination of the policy to develop ESP programs in the National Autonomous University in Mexico in 1974 produced reactions that provided them with the information that (1) multi-lingual specialist glossaries had been prepared for veterinary medicine by an international institution, (2) that an instructor with eight years experience teaching scientific English to animal scientists was available for consultation, and (3) that one ESP program was already being conducted for students of dentistry and another program planned for students of law. To summarize, the dissemination stage ensures that the chances of obtaining valuable information, which might otherwise be overlooked or even unobtainable, are maximized.

PROGRAM DEVELOPMENT STAGE

This stage involves a large number of more or less interrelated activities. These activities include phases during which (1) basic information about the constraints and the potential resources that will have a direct bearing on the nature of the program is gathered and analyzed, (2) the educational objectives of the program are specified, (3) the parameters within which the entire program will be conceived, carried out, and tested/ evaluated are determined, (4) teaching materials, auxiliary aids, and teacher's guides are developed and teachers are trained, and (6) the entire program is evaluated.

Basic Information-Gathering Phase

The purpose of this phase is, on one hand, to ensure that all of the factors that can affect the program, in either beneficial or deleterious ways, are identified, duly weighed, and appropriately taken into consideration. Furthermore, it allows the program developer to specify as clearly and as fully as possible the nature of the needs of those who will benefit from it (the students, the institution, the community) and of those who will be required to teach it.

In determining learners' language needs, care has to be taken to distinguish *real, current needs* (what the student needs the language for now) from *future hypothetical needs* (what the student may want the language for at some unspecified time in the future). Both of these should be distinguished from *student desires* (what the student would *like* to be able to do with the language, independent of the specific requirements of the situation or job for which the needs analysis is being carried out) and *teacher-created needs* (what the teacher imagines is needed or would like to impose on the students). See Table 1.3.

Table 1.3   Types of needs and examples of (imaginary) courses based on these needs

Types of Needs	Example of Course
Future hypothetical needs	A study-skills course in English to prepare students for study in an English-speaking university when only a very small proportion of the students will ever undertake such study.
Teacher-created needs	A reading course based on French literature, because the teacher believes that a goal such as familiarity with the great literary figures is, in itself, worthwhile.
Student desires	A course in conversational Russian in circumstances such that the only opportunity to encounter the language is in the form of written technical information.
Real, current needs	A course in legal French for anglophone students of law in an English-speaking university in a French-speaking region (e.g., Quebec) where there is a legal requirement for all professionals to demonstrate competence in French.

Although the identification of the nature of the learners' needs forms a major component of this phase (this is dealt with in depth in Chapter 2 by Schutz and Derwing), there are other sources from which information must be sought. The community where the learners are operating or will eventually operate is one important source of information. Whether the community is the ethnic or socioeconomic group to which the learners belong, or an institution such as a university research center, or a professional organization, or the work-force the learners will be required to join, it will have a more or less clearly defined set of expectations for the learners as fellow workers and language users. For example, although the learner may specify that the required use of language is "to understand and give oral presentations of scientific papers at international conferences," this ability, for the conference-going community, may include the expectation that a paper-giver will also be willing to defend his or her points of view in a less formal discussion situation with peers. Failure to meet this expectation may reduce the effectiveness of even a superior ability to read a paper intelligibly to a large audience, to a point where the learner cannot function acceptably at conferences. Similarly, a needs assessment might involve gathering information about the reaction of hospital patients to a medical doctor's grammatical errors. Despite the doctor's adequate communicative ability there may be a point above which the frequency or type of grammatical error so reduces the confidence of the patient that an attempt at examination, elicitation of information, or treatment becomes ineffectual, the patient having an expectation of professional competence and accuracy, which is reflected even in his or her reaction to the doctor's linguistic proficiency.

In other situations, parents' expectations of or aspirations for their children, although not explicitly familiar to the teachers or the learners themselves, may have to be taken into consideration in planning a program. Despite a manifest lack of necessity for mastering the written skill early on in a program, parents may so strongly associate all learning with literacy that it could be counterproductive to ignore this expectation to demonstrate learning in a written form.

Basically, two routes are open to the analyst. He or she can elicit information about language needs from the students by means of carefully constructed questionnaires (see Appendix 1 for an example), structured interviews, or checklists; or he or she can elicit information about the actual language use of fluent or native speakers in the situations in which the learner will have to function. Ideally, the analyst will follow both routes, using both the information gained from observation of the language and the language skills used in the target situations as a check on the information obtained from the learner.

At this stage, basic information can be gathered in a number of ways; e.g., questionnaires, structured interviews, or checklists. (See Table 1.4.) Questionnaires (see Chapter 2 by Schutz and Derwing) require skill and caution in their preparation. It is very easy to influence respondents' answers by questions that are poorly worded or subject to interpretation, ambiguously putting the respondent in a good or bad light depending on the answer he or she gives. Moreover, it is frequently very difficult or even impossible to follow up anomalous answers or partially completed questionnaires. Questionnaires are most appropriately used after a series of questions has been piloted with even a small subsample of the population. Such a piloting will provide a fairly clear idea of the variety and range of answers that might be expected from any question, will clarify misunderstandings or ambiguities of wording, and will generally allow the researcher to improve the quality of the information-gathering instrument.

Table 1.4   Some advantages and disadvantages of three kinds of data-gathering instruments

INSTRUMENT	ADVANTAGES	DISADVANTAGES
Questionnaire (to be completed and returned by respondents)	Appears to involve the researcher in less work; i.e., he/she distributes the questionnaires (by post or directly) and simply awaits the return of the completed forms. Permits open-ended questions to be included.	Anomalous responses, misunderstood questions, and unanswered questions may require the researcher to re-administer certain elements of the questionnaire. No check on respondent comprehension of the questions is possible. Only a low percentage of those to whom the questionnaire was directed may reply. Responses to open-ended questions may be difficult to analyze and compare.
Structured interview (administered individually to members of the sample by the researcher)	Interviewer can explain incompletely understood questions if necessary. Interviewer can follow up anomalous answers or answers that suggest a useful line of inquiry previously overlooked. Interviewer can insure that all members of the sample answer all of the questions.	Requires a great deal of time.

(continued on page 10)

Table 1.4 (continued)

Structured interview (continued)	Permits open-ended questions to be included.	
	Permits responses to open-ended questions to be recorded in a more easily analyzed manner.	
Checklist	Very tidy—can be administered directly, even by an untrained research assistant.	Does not permit investigation of anomalous cases.
	Produces neatly comparable data.	Identification of inappropriate categories, scales, or questions is made difficult.
	Produces data that are usually easy to summarize.	

The advantage of structured interviews, although they are more costly to use than postal or otherwise mass-administered questionnaires, is that the interviewer is able to ensure that all questions are adequately understood and answered by each and every respondent, while idiosyncratic responses can be checked out on the spot. A checklist is similar to a questionnaire and is used when virtually all the important factors which require responses are known to the researcher. Whereas a questionnaire or a structured interview usually has at least one open-ended question, to allow for important information that has not been elicited by the structured questions (which usually have a yes/no or scale-type response), a checklist normally has no such open-ended categories. A checklist can be administered to a group or to individuals in an interview situation.

Unless the instruments used in the data-gathering have been well designed and carefully constructed to elicit categories of information that the researchers have predetermined as important, the analysis phase can become a waste of time. The key to successful information-gathering is to determine the purpose of the information, and then to determine how the information will be summarized and by whom, and only after these steps have been taken, to pilot the instrument, improve it, and administer it to the sample. If the researcher assumes that the first step is to gather all possible information about the learner—his or her needs, the uses to which the language might be put, the expectations of the community—before deciding how the information will be analyzed and for what purposes it will be used, this phase is certain to end in frustration and is likely to end in the abandonment of the data.

The outcome of this phase is usually a comprehensive description of the status quo, i.e., the current proficiency (if any) of the learner in the target language, his or her previous exposure to it, and the uses to which the learner will be required to put it.

The principal matter to be resolved is the terms in which these needs will be specified. Is an inventory of linguistic items sufficient or even desirable, or is a more sociolinguistic specification necessary in which the areas of knowledge (scientific, technical) and language skills (translation, reading technical manuals, taking part in boardroom discussions, etc.) as well as the linguistic requirements are detailed? Schutz and Derwing deal with these matters, and the analysis of the information gathered, in more detail in Chapter 2.

Goal Specification Phase

Once the information gathered has been summarized and analyzed so that the program developer can identify the status quo and the set of outcomes desired or behaviors expected, the task of specifying these outcomes in terms of objectives must be carried out.

The question to be answered at this phase is: What should the learner ideally be able to do after successfully completing the instructional program? For example, it might have been determined that a technician should be able *to listen to* oral instructions relating to the operation of specified heavy machinery and *to carry out* these instructions without error; or that a doctor should be able to elicit information from a patient in casualty so that a first diagnosis can be made and the case directed to the most appropriate ward; or that a student should be able to read scientific research papers on animal nutrition, synthesize the information in the light of a specific clinical problem, and suggest orally to colleagues one or more possible lines of action that might lead to a solution of the problem.

These objectives must be written in such a way that there is no ambiguity in their formulation and *description,* so that they can be measured and evaluated. The objectives must state the language skills required, the field of discourse, the level of formality, and the constraints under which this performance will be required (e.g., noisy conditions, on the telephone, with the expectation of interruption, etc.).

These aspects of language and language use are inevitably intimately related, and it is not easy to talk in a detailed way about the desired terminal skills of a program of instruction without touching upon aspects of the register within which the skill is to be demonstrated. There are a number of useful ways of conceptualizing and thereby classifying language in use.

Halliday, McIntosh, and Strevens's discussion (1964) of how we can characterize samples of language in use may be displayed schematically, as in Table 1.5.

Table 1.5   Criteria necessary to define and identify a register

---

Register is defined as the product of:

A. Field of discourse	B. Mode of discourse	C. Style of discourse
—subject matter of the language event (e.g., biology; industrial management)	—the medium employed in the language event (e.g., spoken/written)	—the interpersonal relationships that determine the code used (e.g., formal/casual/intimate/deferential)

Vaughan James (1973) attempts to define language in use by isolating certain components; namely:

a. *Language skills*: Performance in some or all of the four basic skill areas
b. *Special content*: Special terminology, structures, etc., associated with the nonlanguage specialism, such as chemistry, physics, etc.
c. *Functional skills*: The use of language in the performance of tasks associated with operation in the nonlanguage specialisms, e.g., translating, interpreting, taking dictation, handling the telephone, monitoring radio, abstracting press articles, etc.

This is summarized in Figure 1.1.

As pointed out by Halliday, McIntosh, and Strevens (1964), models for the characterization of language in use are not absolute. When the syllabus planner attempts to employ the criteria in order to specify goals and objectives, he or she inevitably discovers that they are capable of

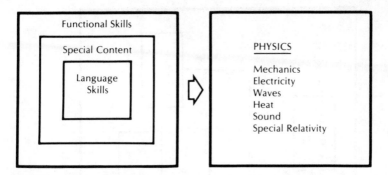

Figure 1.1   Vaughan's components of language in use

being subcategorized and refined and that they eventually tend to overlap considerably.

In an attempt to provide tighter operational guidelines for the specification of learner needs in terms of the syllabus specification required to service these needs, Munby (1978) has provided us with undoubtedly the clearest set of procedures available so far. These are summarized in his Communication Needs Processor, shown in Figure 1.2.

Briefly, the parameters of the model are:

1. Participant—relevant information on the student (e.g., age, sex, mother-tongue, proficiency in the target language, etc.).
2. Purposive Domain—includes both the broad characterization of the type of LSP involved (e.g., occupational, academic, etc.) and the specification of the discipline or field of work.
3. Setting—information concerning the spatial (e.g., hotel, factory, etc.) and temporal (e.g., when the target language is required, for how long, and how frequently) aspects of the physical setting as well as details of the psycho-social setting(s) (e.g., culturally similar to urban/rural, aggressive/harmonious, etc.) in which language will be used.
4. Interaction—with whom the participant will have to communicate, and the relationships obtaining.
5. Instrumentality—medium (spoken/written, receptive/productive); mode (monologue/dialogue); channel (face-to-face, telephone, print, public address system, etc.).
6. Dialect—refers principally to the variety of the target language required (e.g., Continental French or Quebec French; British or American English; Peninsular or Central American Spanish, etc.).
7. Target Level—specifies the dimensions (size, complexity, range,

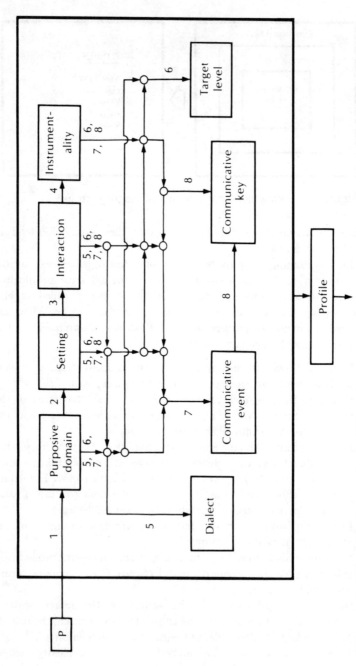

Figure 1.2 Munby's Communication Needs Processor

delicacy, speed, flexibility) and the conditions (tolerance of error, stylistic failure, reference, repetition, and hesitation) of the learner's target performance.

8. Communicative Event—what the participant has to be able to do, receptively or productively in terms of the activity (e.g., note-taking from lectures, writing up an experiment, etc.) and the subject matter (topic).

9. Communicative Key—the attitudinal tones the learner is required to master (happy/unhappy, frivolous/serious, formal/informal, respectful/disrespectful, lenient/severe, etc.).

The appropriate use of these parameters provides a very detailed communication needs profile of the student or group for whom the syllabus is being devised. At this point, the needs profile is translated into a statement of the specific language skills that are required by the learner. Munby's model specifies language skills as being composed of an "operational element" (e.g., understanding, expressing, interpreting, recognizing, identifying, etc.), which dominates a communicative feature (e.g., sounds in connected speech, attitudinal meaning, explicitly stated information, relations within the sentence, etc.), which in turn may dominate any extension of the feature (e.g., reduction of unstressed vowels, pitch range, making inferences, elements of sentence structure, etc.). His taxonomy consists of almost three hundred subskills grouped into fifty-four categories. It is undoubtedly the most detailed specification of language skills available and, used in connection with the information obtained from the Communication Needs Processor, permits the syllabus planner to specify the sequential goals of a language program in minute detail. Munby's approach probably has to be followed carefully and respectfully in practice before its value—which is considerable—is fully appreciated.

At this point, the program planner now has relevant information as to the present level of proficiency and knowledge of the students, and the target level of proficiency and knowledge required of the students. He or she is now faced with the task of determining by what means the objectives can most effectively and efficiently be achieved in the time available and given the intensity of instruction possible. It is important to note that if the desired outcome is unattainable, given the constraints of time, intensity of instruction, and amount of finance or number of personnel with which the project is expected to be carried out, this state of affairs should be formally acknowledged and communicated to the appropriate authority. It has not infrequently happened that LSP programs have been brought into disrepute by planners striving to achieve manifestly impossible goals. If it becomes obvious that the desired goals cannot possibly be attained, then the only practical and honest course open to the program planner is to persuade the client to accept modified goals or to abandon the project altogether as unfeasible. This is then a *Compromise Stage*.

Production Phase

On the basis of the information provided by the needs analysis, the materials writer may select appropriate samples of the target language that adequately represent the characteristics of the target language and the associated demands it will place upon the user. For example, if the area of knowledge is animal nutrition and the learner will be required to read advanced textbooks and research papers on the subject, then the language samples will have to adequately represent such textbooks and research papers. If the area of knowledge is banking, and the learner will be required to explain different banking procedures, to complete the associated paper work, and to show professional courtesy to bank clients, then representative language samples from these areas of use will be required.

The Selection of the Target Language Upon which the Instructional Materials will be Based. For many LSP programs no adequate nor even suitable materials exist in ready-to-use form. This means that the materials writer may have to produce the instructional materials from scratch. The first step is likely to be the selection of a set of texts, oral or written, which are representative of the language that the learner will be required to master. Hence it is important to have an adequate classification system within which to describe the target language (see Chapter 4 by Palmer). Inadequate criteria are often used to describe textual materials, which may result, for example, in recorded versions of written texts being used to train students in listening comprehension, or popular science articles being used as training texts for students who are required to read scientific reports.

Syllabus Specification. The preparation of a syllabus for the second-language program requires that the target objectives and language that the learner will be expected to master be broken down into an optimally sequenced series of teaching and learning points. Exposure to the target language alone does not satisfy the expectations of the adult learner; nor does it make use of the advantages we assume occur from organizing and sequencing instruction in such a way that facilitates learning. Despite expectations to the contrary, communicative language syllabuses (often going under the names "semantic," "functional," or "notional") still require a conscious linguistic structuring on the part of the planner.

However, although communicative syllabuses still require that significant grammatical generalizations be sequenced and presented in such a way that they can be noted by the learner, they have an additional feature. In addition to the grammatical point or points being focused upon in any given unit or lesson, the communicative ends to which these points are utilized are also made clear. Hence, not only would the structure involving "if and present simple and will" be presented as a grammatical generalization worthy of the learner's attention, but it would also be used in such a way as to show that it is a warning in one case:

> Mixing water and acid can be dangerous. *If you pour water into a beakerful of acid an explosion will occur.* A safer procedure is to add the acid to the water.

and an exhortation in another:

> Hard work usually pays off. *If you learn the elements in the periodic chart you will have mastered very valuable information.*

Thus, an important formal (in this case, grammatical) feature of the language is presented in such a way as to make the generalization meaningful to the specific group of learners involved.

An adequate syllabus for an LSP course would list the steps in terms of the grammatical, lexical, and communicative generalizations required to reach the specified objectives of the program.

The selection of the teaching points from the adequate language sample is carried out in such a way as to incorporate in each unit of presentation one or more significant generalizations about the language and how it is used.

Classroom Procedures: Strategies and Associated Techniques. Deciding upon the kinds of exercises, teaching strategies, classroom organization, and auxiliary materials or equipment to be employed is a phase of the materials development stage that requires not only linguistic knowledge but also considerable teaching experience and a flair for creativity. The creativity and innovation, however, have to be informed by what is possible, practical, and acceptable to both learner and instructor. Most teachers appreciate a certain freedom of action, within the limits of the syllabus, to develop techniques that suit their personalities, their preferred styles of teaching, and their perception of the learner's reactions to the learning task. Rarely are materials that are totally prescriptive in their exploitation looked upon favorably by teachers. Moreover, most learners have some idea, however personal it may be, of what they should be doing in order to learn a language. Both teacher attitudes and learner expectations can be modified and modeled to some extent by ensuring that the teachers and the students understand the course objectives and rationale underlying the materials, techniques, and associated classroom procedures. Teachers can receive special training sessions in the use of the new materials. It is necessary, however, to obtain information from both teachers and students at regular intervals during the trial period. Information obtained by interviewing teachers and students, and by observing the materials being used in class, and by having the teachers and students complete questionnaires or checklists that relate to their perceptions of the effectiveness of the exercises, techniques, and strategies can be used to adjust the material so that their form and content are highly acceptable (see Appendix 2).

The classroom procedures for the appropriate exploitation of the materials are then selected so that they present and practice these significant generalizations for the learner in a way that is meaningful and insightful. As well as judging how meaningful they are to the learner, how successfully they can be used by the teacher, and how enjoyable they are for teacher and student, it is also important to determine the extent to which they generate the kind of language and behavior that has been identified as the objective.

It is useful to subject all exercise types used in the materials to scrutiny according to the following checklist:

1. Expected outcome in terms of target language skill. Munby's list would be most useful here.
2. As precise a statement as possible of the language knowledge the learner would be required to possess in order to complete the exercise successfully; that is, an explicit statement of the linguistic point or points without which the exercise cannot be adequately or correctly performed.
3. A statement of the precise activity in which the student would be involved while carrying out and completing the exercise successfully.

The materials writer may discover, more frequently than expected, that some of his or her exercises are not contributing directly to the goals established for the lesson. Action can then be taken and the exercises altered, or the sequence of instruction modified, in order to improve the efficacy of the exercises.

At this point, it is essential that the teachers selected to use novel, special-purpose instructional materials be adequately briefed as to the principles according to which they were written, to the anticipated outcomes in terms of what the student is expected to learn, and to the ways in which the materials might best be exploited in class. Unless teachers understand and are sympathetic to the nature and goals of new materials and techniques, it is unlikely that they will be used enthusiastically or well.

Trial Phase

There are two major types of evaluation used in program development. The first is *formative evaluation,* carried out on a day-to-day basis during the Production Phase to determine the effectiveness of, for example, a teaching unit, a method of presentation, or even an individual exercise, and to provide immediate feedback to the materials writer so that weaknesses can be avoided and improvements in the materials constantly incorporated (see Chapter 7 by Bachman). The second type is *summative evaluation,* carried out at the end of the trial teaching period in order to determine the extent to which the goals for the new program are achieved.

The major purpose of formative evaluation is to gather information on every aspect of the program, e.g., its general aims, the specific objectives, the experimental materials and auxiliary teaching aids, the trial teaching, the teacher-training associated with the new syllabus, etc., in order to facilitate decision-making which will affect the shape of the program as it is being put together. The effect is to improve all aspects of the program as its development proceeds so that the final plan is in an optimal form for field-trialling on an extensive basis—if indeed the program is to be used extensively. Relevant information is sought from experts in the field, teachers, parents, community representatives and indeed any source that is likely to be affected directly or indirectly by the new program. Data from classroom observations and progress tests are, of course, also sought and taken into consideration.

Summative evaluation, on the other hand, because it tends to provide a picture of the extent to which the entire program has or has not been successful in achieving its goals, usually serves as a basis for accountability to the responsible body in authority, such as a school board, the curriculum committee of an institution, or a Ministry of Education.

As second generation, special-purpose, language-teaching programs appear and are trialled, so techniques for the summative evaluation of these programs will develop. However, to date, the enthusiasm surrounding LSP program creation and development has tended to overshadow evaluation activites; and empirical evaluation studies, formative or summative, are scarce in the applied linguistic literature. The best recourse the LSP program evaluator has at the moment are the several volumes on the evaluation of general educational programs, which are more familiar to traditional main-line educationalists than to applied linguists.

APPENDIX 1.1

Example of a Student Needs Questionnaire*

AURAL COMPREHENSION

Purpose of this questionnaire. Tuition in English language is available to overseas postgraduate students who require it. In order to provide the most effective tuition we need to know, firstly, the kinds of situations in which you find difficulty; and secondly, the kinds of difficulty you find. By completing this questionnaire you will be giving valuable assistance toward the provision of relevant and effective tuition. Thank you for your cooperation.

NOTE: The questionnaire deals with the English you need to *listen to* during your studies in the university; it does not deal with problems you may meet outside; for example, shopping, travel, or social occasions.

Section 1: BACKGROUND INFORMATION

1.1   Name_____

1.2   Age_____

1.3   Mother tongue _____

1.4   University department_____

1.5   Qualification for which you are studying _____

_____

1.6   How long have you been studying in *this university*?

_____ years _____ months

---

*The Editors gratefully acknowledge James W. Morrison's permission to adapt this questionnaire from his M. Ed. thesis, *An Investigation of Problems in Listening Comprehension encountered by overseas students in the first year of postgraduate studies in sciences in the University of Newcastle-upon-Tyne and the implications for teaching,* University of Newcastle-upon-Tyne, 1974.

1.7   How long have you been studying in *this country*?

_____ years _____ months

1.8   Are you sponsored? (e.g., by Fulbright, Ford Foundation, your own government)

a. YES/NO _____

b. If YES, name of sponsoring body _____

1.9   Before commencing study at this university, did you attend a language school in this country?

a. YES/NO _____

b. If YES, how long was the course? _____ months

1.10 Did you have any formal qualification in English before you came to this country?

a. YES/NO _____

b. If YES, give brief details (e.g., national school certificate, proficiency certificate, etc.) _____

_____

1.11 Do you attend the Language Centre?

a. YES/NO _____

b. If YES, approximately how many hours per week? _____ hours

Section 2: *LISTENING SITUATIONS*

Do you find difficulty in understanding in any of the situations listed below, in which you are expected to learn by listening?

In column A, write YES or NO opposite each item; if you write YES opposite more than one item, indicate the *one* that is most important by drawing a circle round the answer, like this, (YES) .

In column B, write an estimate of the number of hours you spend each week engaged in the activity.

		A	B
2.1	Formal lectures (during which students are not expected to interrupt or to ask questions)	____	____
2.2	Informal lectures (during which it is permitted to ask questions)	____	____
2.3	Seminar or tutorial groups (during which questions and discussion from students are necessary and expected)	____	____

2.4 Demonstrations (by technician or demonstrator) _____ _____

2.5 Individual discussion with tutor or instructor _____ _____

2.6 Other (e.g., farm walk, factory visit—please write in the situation)_____

_____

_____ _____ _____

Section 3: LISTENING PROBLEMS

3.1 Did any of the items in the following list cause you difficulty when you *started* your studies in this university?

Answer YES or NO; if you choose more than one YES, please remember to encircle the *one* which is most important (this applies to each section)

Sound

a. Speaker talking too fast _____

b. Speaker's accent or pronunciation difficult _____

c. Difficulty in hearing (e.g., speaker not loud enough, or outside noise interference) _____

Meaning

d. Recognizing words from the stream of sound _____

e. Realizing where sentences begin and end _____

f. Following the argument (that is, connecting what the speaker is saying *now* with what he or she has already said in previous sentences) _____

3.2 Is there any listening problem not mentioned above that caused you difficulty when you started your studies? Please write it below. (If possible, give an example of what you mean.)_____

_____

_____

3.3 Which of the items in the following list cause you difficulty *now*? Write YES or NO opposite each item; if you choose more than one YES remember to encircle the *one* that is most important.

a. Speaker talking too fast _____

b. Speaker's accent or pronunciation difficult _____

c. Difficulty in hearing (e.g., speaker not loud enough, or outside noise interference) _____

d. Recognizing words from the stream of sound _____

e. Realizing where sentences begin and end _____

f. Following the argument (that is, connecting what the speaker is saying *now* with what he or she has already said in previous sentences) _____

g. Is there any listening problem not mentioned above that causes you difficulty now? Please write it below. (If possible, give an example of what you mean.) _____

_____

_____

_____

Section 4: DISTRIBUTION

4.1 Does the same difficulty occur in *all* listening situations of the same type? That is, if a difficulty occurs in a lecture, does it occur in *all* lectures; if a difficulty occurs in a tutorial, does it occur in all tutorials?

(Check the appropriate column opposite each item.)

	Difficulty occurs:				
	always 1	almost always 2	sometimes 3	almost never 4	never 5
a. Seminars or tutorials	___	___	___	___	___
b. Individual discussion	___	___	___	___	___
c. Informal lectures	___	___	___	___	___

    d. Formal lectures   ___   ___   ____   ___   ___

    e. Demonstrations   ___   ___   ____   ___   ___

    f. Other (e.g., factory
       visits, etc.)   ___   ___   ____   ___   ___

4.2   For the items checked in columns 2, 3, and 4 of the previous question, please indicate whether the greater difficulty is caused by (a) or (b) following (check one or the other).

    a. The speaker (that is, *how* he or she speaks—voice, accent, etc.) ___

    b. The subject content (that is, *what* he or she is speaking about) ___

4.3   Look at the items you have marked in columns 2, 3, and 4 of question 4.1. For those in which you think the greater difficulty is caused by the *speaker,* which of the following items make one speaker easier to understand than another?

    Check the item or items you choose; if you choose more than one, indicate the most important *one* by encircling the checkmark, like this,

    a. Speed   _____

    b. Loudness   _____

    c. Pronunciation or accent   _____

    d. The way in which the speaker stresses
       important words   _____

    e. The speaker does not use idioms or slang
       expressions too much   _____

    f. The speaker does not use very complicated
       sentences   _____

    g. The way in which the speaker repeats the
       important points   _____

4.4   Is there any other factor, not mentioned above, that makes one speaker easier to understand than another? If so, please write it below.

_____

_____

_____

_____

Section 5: NOTE-TAKING

5.1 In which of these activities do you take notes? (Check the appropriate item or items.)

    a. Formal lectures   _____

    b. Informal lectures   _____

    c. Seminars or tutorials   _____

    d. Demonstrations   _____

    e. Individual discussions   _____

    f. Other (e.g. factory visits, etc.)   _____

5.2 In which language do you usually take your notes?_____

5.3 Do you choose this language for reasons of:

    a. Speed in note-taking   _____

    b. To improve your command of the language   _____

    c. To cut out loss of time in translation   _____

    d. To improve speed of translation   _____

    e. Any other reason (please write it below)

    _____

    _____

5.4 Do you find that your notes are satisfactory? (Check *one* of the following choices.)

    a. Always   _____

    b. Almost always   _____

    c. Sometimes   _____

    d. Almost never   _____

    e. Never   _____

5.5 Do you experience any of the following difficulties in taking notes? Write YES or NO opposite each item; if you write more than one YES, please indicate the *one* that is most important by encircling the YES.

    a. Recognizing what is important and worth noting down   _____

    b. Trying to write too much   _____

    c. Finding suitable abbreviations   _____

    d. Not being able to write fast enough   _____

5.6 Is there any other difficulty you have in taking notes, not included in the above list? If so, please write it below.

_____

_____

5.7 Whenever your notes are *not* satisfactory, is it because of any of the following? Write YES or NO opposite each item. If you write more than one YES, encircle the *one* that is most important.

    a. You miss too many important points   _____

    b. You try to write too much   _____

    c. You don't write enough   _____

    d. Your notes are too badly organized   _____

5.8 Is there any other reason that may cause your notes to be unsatisfactory, not mentioned above? If so, please write it below.

_____

_____

5.9 Would any of the following items help to improve your note-taking? Write YES or NO opposite each item; if you write more than one YES, indicate the item that would help most by encircling the YES.

    a. Previous training in listening to native
       English speakers   _____

    b. Previous training in note-taking   _____

    c. The speaker speaking more slowly   _____

    d. Knowing more words   _____

5.10 Is there any other item that might help to improve your note-taking? If so, please write it below.

_____

_____

APPENDIX 1.2

Example of a Teacher Feedback Questionnaire

LESSON EVALUATION FORM

Please fill in the information requested below.

1. *GENERAL INFORMATION ON LESSON*
1.1 Lesson reference number: _____
1.2 Number of lesson forms handed out: _____
1.3 Date(s) used: _____
1.4 Approximate class time (hour/minutes) dedicated to the lesson in class: _____

2. *TEXT AND SPECIFIC EXERCISES*
2.1 The general difficulty in this lesson (text and specific exercises) seemed: —higher than in preceding lessons
                    —about the same as in preceding lessons
                    —lower than in preceding lessons
2.2 Students' problems (if any) in doing this lesson (text and specific exercises) where especially related to: (Please specify the difficulties within each category)
    a. Sentence structure
    b. Grammatical forms
    c. The meaning of technical vocabulary
    d. The meanings of common English words
    e. Other, please specify
2.3 (Please specify exercise number or letter in the following responses)
    a. Students had *unusual difficulty* in doing:
        Exercise(s): _____
        Reasons: _____
    b. Exercise(s) _____
        _____ seemed *too easy*.
        Reason: _____
    c. Students showed *special interest* in
        Exercise(s) _____
        Reason: _____

d. Exercise(s) _____

_____ seemed *boring/unchallenging*
to students.

2.4   The sequence/order in which the exercises are presented in this lesson
seemed:

−adequate

−inadequate

If inadequate, please indicate a more suitable sequence and give
reasons for your suggestions

a. _____   Reason _____

b. _____   _____

(etc.) _____   _____

3.   *GENERAL STUDENT INTEREST IN THIS LESSON*
(Please check *one* option in each of the following items and give
reasons for your opinion)

−high

3.1   General student interest in this lesson seemed: −satisfactory

−low

Reasons: _____

3.2   Student attention to the exercises in this lesson seemed:

−to vary considerably

−to remain fairly constant

3.3   Students seem to feel that the reading material in this lesson is:

relevant

to their academic interests

irrelevant

Reason: _____

4.   Students' criticism of this lesson. (Please solicit, and describe briefly
and precisely below and on the reverse side of this page.)

_____

5.   Teachers' criticism and suggestions for improving this lesson. (Use
space below and reverse side of this page.)

_____

Note: Please return this completed form with the corresponding
annotated copy of the lesson.

2

The Problem of Needs Assessment in English for Specific Purposes: Some Theoretical and Practical Considerations

Noel W. Schutz
American Language Academy
University of Tampa

Bruce L. Derwing
Department of Linguistics
University of Alberta

In recent years there has been, in programs in Second Languages (SL), a greater focus of interest on the specialized area of Languages for Special Purposes (LSP), particularly in the subfield of Languages for Science and Technology (LST). This focus has come out of a growing awareness that the language needs of students in the highly specialized fields of science and technology—as in many other professional areas of business and industry—go beyond the standard format of ordinary course offerings in SL, and that certain, perhaps major, adjustments in orientation, methods, and materials may be required to satisfy these needs.

These developments, in turn, have given a new importance and even a sense of urgency to the whole question of the assessment of course goals and student needs. In the first place, it is difficult to disagree with Wilkins's view that the "first principle" of a sound approach to language teaching is "to know what the objectives of teaching are," and this means that, as far as circumstances allow, "it is necessary to predict what kinds of language skills will be of greatest value to the learner" (Wilkins, 1974:58). This implies, of course, that at least a preliminary analysis of learner needs and expectations will be a prerequisite to program development in any language-teaching situation, whether for "general" or for "specific" purposes (cf. Bachman and Strick, 1978). Nevertheless, the problem of needs assessment and evaluation seems to have received surprisingly little attention until quite recently, apart from the administration of standard FL proficiency tests. Thus, as Palmer and Mackay describe the situation:

> Many well-intentioned language programs purporting to provide "English for Businessmen," "French for Engineers," "German for Scientists," have foundered because either no consideration was given to the actual use the learner intended to make of the language or because the list of uses drawn up by the course designer was based on imagination rather than an objective assessment of the learner's situation, and proved to be inaccurate and in many cases entirely inappropriate to his real needs. (Palmer and Mackay, 1978:3)

The problem, therefore, as Perren has put it, is that:

> There seems to be some danger ... of making imaginative and sometimes spurious assumptions about categories of need simply because we have no adequate descriptions of the use of language in defined circumstances by mother-tongue speakers, let alone by second-language users, and certainly insufficiently reliable information to provide practical inventories of check lists or items to be taught. (Perren, 1974:9)

This situation is surprising, since it would seem that most language planners in the past have bypassed a logically necessary first step: they have presumed to set about going somewhere without first determining whether or not their planned destination was reasonable or proper. From another point of view, however, the situation is not in the least bit surprising. For language teachers and planners are required to be very pragmatic people who have a job to do which simply cannot wait for the tools and background research that might be available in "the best of all possible worlds." Furthermore, it is quite obvious from even the little research done so far that the systematic assessment of learner needs and expectations is going to be a very complicated and difficult enterprise indeed, at least if the results are to be of sufficiently high quality to afford any genuine benefit to language teachers and their students. But whether this long delay in coming to grips with the problem is understandable or excusable or not, the upshot is that the enterprise of needs assessment in LSP (in all FL programs generally) is still very much in its infancy today.

RECENT THEORETICAL DEVELOPMENTS

Recent trends in needs assessment have concentrated almost exclusively on individual rather than on group needs. Jordan (1977), for example, provides a taxonomy of methods that have been used to provide information about the individual "student profile" (especially for the type of student who comes from abroad to undertake specialized English-language training in an English-speaking country). He includes proficiency tests, self-assessment tasks, live observation by teacher, surveys and questionnaires, and finally, more detailed basic (controlled) research on problems already known to exist. One outcome of these efforts, of course, has been, just as Crymes (1978) reported, a recognition that many of the "language" problems that foreign learners experience are as much sociological as linguistic in character (see also Spolsky, 1971). This recognition, in turn, has recently given rise to a host of studies that effectively reverse the old set of priorities: Where once it was thought that the linguistic structures were the key factors and the circumstances of use merely tangential, if relevant at all, a new orthodoxy seems now in the making, which asserts that a detailed analysis of the situations of language use is a prerequisite even to the selection of the particular linguistic forms or structures that ought to be taught.

Although exemplars of this new trend are now beginning to appear in virtually every corner of the field (see Bojar, 1965, p. 2, for an early illustration), the most extreme (and hence most definitive) illustration of the approach is probably that of John Munby. In his chapter on "Processing Profiles of Communication Needs" (1978), Munby expresses his basic agreement with Hymes and others (1972) that—

> there are rules of [language] use without which the rules of grammar woud be useless. . . . In other words, the specification of communication needs is prior [even] to the selection of speech functions or rhetorical acts to be taught. (Gumperz and Hymes, eds., 1972:15)

Thus, notes Essebaggers, before the language program can be most usefully determined by language teachers—

> field work needs to be done to find out: (a) a description of the language needs in real situations, (b) a description of the types of tasks or activities people need to engage in in order to function in particular situations, and (c) a description of the groups and individuals who need or want to function in these situations and what their language learning ability, motivation, etc., is (Essebaggers' contribution to discussion, in Mackay, 1973:286).

Just what, then, are the dimensions or parameters of Munby's concept of communication needs? He mentions nine, which are summarized here for convenience:

PROFILE OF COMMUNICATIVE NEEDS

1. Personal	Culturally significant information about the individual, such as language background
2. Purpose	Occupational or educational objective for which the target language is required
3. Setting	Physical and psychosocial setting in which the target language is required
4. Interaction variables	Such as the role relationships to be involved in the target language use
5. Medium, mode, and channel	Communicative means
6. Dialects	Information on dialects to be utilized
7. Target level	Level of competence required in the target language
8. Anticipated communicative events	Micro- and macro-activities
9. Key	The specific manner in which communication is actually carried out

It is hardly necessary to point out here that, for all its obvious virtues, such a full-scale assault on the problem of needs assessment is rather ambitious, to say the least, particularly when one realizes that even its most complete specification for a given participant contains no specification whatsoever "of the actual language forms that will realize these needs" (Munby, 1977:20). External considerations thus make the fully detailed Munby-type investigation quite impractical for most program planners, at least for the time being. While this should not deter us from attempting such research, it is doubtful that the full results will be available for a good long time; meanwhile we have programs to develop and materials to write.

SOME PRAGMATIC CONSIDERATIONS

Van Ek (1975) brings the problem closer to our immediate reality. He notes that individual needs will undoubtedly vary widely, "yet organized education can only cater for the individual learner if he can be grouped with other learners to form a sufficiently large class to justify the efforts and finances required to satisfy his needs" (p. 2). For Van Ek, therefore, the problem is not so much one of specifying in minute detail the "micro-needs" of each individual FL learner, but rather the much more feasible one of indentifying large overlapping categories of needs which are found to be shared by substantial numbers of such students. Nor might it be always necessary to aim at the inculcation of a full range of linguistic skills to satisfy these needs, since a very basic or "threshold" level might well suffice for most purposes (cf. Davis, 1977:36).

Pragmatic considerations thus dictate that the new enthusiasm to base language programs on a prior careful specification of communication needs ought to be mollified in at least the following two directions. First, since not all *individual* needs can realistically be satisfied by any program, the best to be hoped for is the development of a number of alternative instructional "tracks" which incorporate very broadly groups of students with somewhat different occupational, professional, or educational goals; and second, since it is not the place of the language program to teach an entire academic subject per se, course goals must be limited to the establishment of some realistic "threshold" level of language competence which will insure academic success from the standpoint of language skills (though not from the standpoint of academic knowledge, motivation, intelligence, or other factors). In short, there are practical limits to the kind of "specialization" that ESP programs can realistically be expected to achieve.

This brings us to the question of the kinds of programs for which assessment instruments might practically be developed. There are four major types in common use today.

Home Study by Individuals. This would require the development of both texts and tapes. The same objections as to details raised above are particularly relevant here. Texts cannot be made too specific for pure marketing reasons, since they need to be of value to a specified minimum population in order for the publisher to realize a profit. Detailed syllabuses for very narrow specialization areas will not meet this economic requirement. Planners must determine the major categories of users and develop texts and tapes that can be used by students across a variety of occupational specialties. Needs assessment can therefore be directed at common problems shared by large classes of potential students, rather than at the specific problems or interests of individual learners.

Service Courses in English. These are courses in English offered by subject-area schools or by companies that recognize the need for improved English competence on the part of their students or employees. These schools or companies might be situated either in the foreign country or in an English-speaking country. The detailed specification of needs is generally less practical in the former case than in the latter, as the result of a limited native-speaking faculty and attendant heavy reliance on tests and tapes developed in English-speaking countries. Some of the larger American companies with worldwide branches could conceivably indulge in large-scale research to develop programs specifically suited to their own particular needs, and it is in this area that the detailed specification route may have its greatest opportunity for implementation. To date, however, most companies have tended to rely on ready-made programs and materials developed on the outside.

Standard English Language Programs. These are programs that provide exclusive English language instruction, whether at home or abroad or whether in conjunction with a college or university or on a private basis (such as the American Language Academy). Such programs tend to be of three basic types: (a) intensive (from twenty-one to thirty hours of instruction per week), (b) semi-intensive (eleven to twenty hours per week), or (c) part-time (from three to ten hours per week). Most of these programs are committed to a "general" approach to English language training and do not have the funds or other resources to develop highly specialized English courses.

Special Programs in ESP. There have been a few successful specialized ESP programs, usually offered during the summer months, and some groups, such as the American Language Academy, Reading, Colchester, Pathway, ELF, etc., have developed resource centers of ESP materials so as to offer special technical English courses when the demand warrants it. Again, the difficulties are the myriad educational and occupational objectives of students and the associated difficulty of gathering together a sufficiently large body of students with homogeneous interests to make such courses economically feasible.

EIGHT ESSENTIAL STEPS TO NEEDS EVALUATION: A CASE STUDY

Given such a diverse set of programs and goals, where does one begin with the problem of the assessment of needs? The following proposals were developed on the basis of a survey conducted by the authors in the Republic of China (Derwing, Schutz, and Yang, 1977), constrained only by the broad range of interests denoted by the term "science and technology." Our project consisted of eight discrete phases, which would seem to constitute an absolute minimum for any needs assessment effort worthy of the name. These eight phases were as follows:

1. Defining the purpose
2. Delimiting the target population
3. Delimiting the parameters of investigation
4. Selecting the information-gathering instrument
5. Collection of the data
6. Analysis of the results
7. Interpretation of the results
8. Critique of the project

Defining the Purpose. This may seem a self-evident step, but one of the most common flaws of survey-type work is to leap into a project before its goals are clearly established. Is it basic psycholinguistic or sociolinguistic research? Is it theoretically motivated assessment and evaluation, or is it oriented toward the needs of specific programs? The more precisely the investigator(s) can determine the objective in mind, the more useful will be the results.

In the case of the Taiwan project, for example, the vaguely stated request was to discover information that would be useful to foreign language departments (for English) in developing programs that would serve the interests of Taiwan by more relevant course work or off-campus programs for science and technology and business and industry. It was to be oriented to general overall needs and perspectives rather than to specific tasks and skills, yet we were requested to establish whether the English language needs of science and technology students (or practicing professionals) differed in any important ways from those of the general educated population. Apart from this, however, our goals were not at all well defined before the actual research got underway and the results of our project have suffered accordingly.

Delimiting the Target Population. This, of course, is an undertaking concomitant with the first phase. For example, in the case of the Taiwan project it was impractical both from a monetary position and from time considerations to sample nonacademic sectors (such as factories, businesses, and the like), or to extend the comparison of ESP needs and general English language needs beyond one major university campus. Again, time considerations were the primary factors. To offset this lack, however, two standard English language programs were surveyed: a private language school provided a student body in which there were a number of businessmen and non-EST college students bound for the United States, and a semi-official language school which provided students who were active professionals rather than college-age students, but who were also bound for advanced technical training in the United States.

The result was that three different populations were surveyed:

1. The student body and faculty of a college of science and technology containing only two departments which did not fall into this category
2. The students of a private language school with nearly 50 percent of its students slated for colleges and universities in the United States, businessmen actively engaged in trade with Americans and the United States, professional technicians or engineers, and unemployed young people with ambitions in one of these areas
3. The students of a semi-official language school, all professional engineers designated for advanced training in the United States

This population was sufficient to make inferences with respect to some of the initial aims of the study; it also offered some insight into other areas. In the analysis of the investigation it will be seen that a number of ESP needs were touched upon and at least some significant results obtained.

Delimiting the Parameters of Investigation. An early example of how parameters can be systematically established is from Schutz's research in Arizona under the direction of Carl Voegelin in a language situation survey of Arizona as part of the Southwest culture area (Voegelin, Voegelin, and Schutz, 1967). Before the investigation began, considerable discussion was given to recent work in sociolinguistics and the relevant literature had been read. This provided a theoretical and methodological foundation on which a detailed interview schedule could be based. The purpose of the investigation was determined to be that of isolating the factors relevant to the "linguistic situation" in the broad sense, but the study developed the notion of "linguistic ecology," which later provided Einar Haugen with a concept for his *The Ecology of Language* (1972). The success of the effort can be credited to the fact that enough research had preceded the survey to make it possible to construct a detailed interview schedule containing information of personal, communal, external, sexual, generational, and other data, which was arranged into an interviewing matrix. This study was carried out among the Indian tribes of Arizona and several large minority groups (such as the Basque and Japanese).

In the Taiwan project the questionnaire used grew out of the investigators' own background and recent readings in sociolinguistic research on ESP needs, supplemented by on-the-spot, common-sense "intuitions." Thus the larger portions of the questionnaire turned out to be oriented to questions about the four traditional language skills and certain functional tasks related to them and to professional and occupational undertakings. The survey would have been more adequate if considerably more planning could have gone into the parameters of the investigation. The following are the categories of questions asked of the population surveyed:

a. General background (7 percent of total questions)
b. Occupational speciality or academic field (1 percent of total)
c. English language background (14 percent)
d. Attitudinal and motivational factors (8 percent)
e. Relevance of English to use in occupational or professional field (10 percent)
f. Basic English language skills (25 percent)
g. Functional registers and job tasks (20 percent)
h. Course content and methods of instruction (13 percent)
i. Reaction to project (1 percent)

Except for the questions relating to functional registers, job tasks, and basic English language skills, this was essentially a shotgun technique to elicit a broad spectrum of information on a variety of presumably relevant topics. It seriously begs for follow-up research to confirm its major findings and to extend the range of coverage to parameters that may well have been originally overlooked or inadequately treated. To be fair to the project, however, it should be recognized that this was largely a pioneering effort which was operating in an effective theoretical and methodological vacuum, so perhaps little more could have been expected of the project at that time.

Selecting the Information-Gathering Instrument. In a groundbreaking exploratory study such as the Taiwan project, a questionnaire was the suitable data-gathering instrument, since what was sought was a great deal of general information from a large number of subjects, in order to establish statistically signifcant trends. In the case of the Arizona project, however, the use of a written questionnaire was precluded by the lack of a common language and severe literacy limitations. In any event, where practical, the detailed oral interview has some very definite advantages over the written questionnaire; foremost among them, perhaps, the flexibility it permits the interviewer to pursue unanticipated or particularly interesting lines of inquiry as they develop. Still other instruments, such as the case study, the controlled experiment, or the simple diagnostic test may be preferable as the circumstances warrant. In general, therefore, the scope and objectives of the inquiry will largely determine the nature of the investigation, and hence the choice of the most appropriate investigatory instrument.

Collection of the Data. This is the phase in which the decisions previously arrived at are actually implemented—a seemingly straight-forward matter, yet one whose difficulties must to some extent be anticipated if the research is to be completed under the constraints initially assumed. In the case of the Taiwan project, for example, there were six major tasks involved in the information-gathering phase. These were (a) the translation of the entire questionnaire into Chinese (and subsequent verification of the translation by an independent source), (b) the printing of the translated version, (c) the orientation of class leaders at the Chinese university (and of the English language teachers at the language schools) as to the purpose and context of the questionnaire and the method of distribution and retrieval, (d) the distribution of the questionnaire to all of the subjects in the three populations, (e) the retrieval of the questionnaire and its return to a central office, and, finally, (f) the tabulation of the raw data and its processing into a form appropriate for the next phase. Needless to say, a considerable period of precious time passed from the date on which the English version of the questionnaire was completed and the date when all of the preliminary processing of the data was completed.

Analysis of the Results. Computer-assisted analysis is needed for most surveys of large populations and/or for questionnaires or interviews that involve a large number of questions. In Taiwan, the basic data were coded and punched onto cards for preliminary computer analysis at the host university, and the cards were later sent to the University of Alberta for additional analysis with the help of the more advanced computer service facilities available there. For those few open-ended questions that were included in the Taiwan survey—and for all of the data collected in the Arizona project—categorization and analysis had to be done by hand. This is very time-consuming, to be sure, but the kind of information collected by open-ended questions often cannot be gained any other way, so the inconvenience is unavoidable. In an extensive survey of military officers returning from duty in Taiwan (Schutz and Wicker, 1968), the open-ended portions of the questionnaire proved to be the most valuable in developing cross-cultural confrontation exercises for television, as they enumerated literally hundreds of case studies in intercultural conflict. While the majority of the responses were tabulated by computer, they proved to be much less useful for the pedagogical purposes for which the survey was designed—the development of an intercultural orientation program curriculum.

Interpretation of the Results. This is the crux of the entire operation and is, accordingly, the most difficult and challenging phase. In the instance of the Taiwan project, it entailed hours of poring over computer printouts and a final period of trying to figure out just what it was that we had learned. It was shown in our discussion above, that there were nine separate categories of questions represented in our survey, but this taxonomy was developed only after the fact. There is subjectivity in these interpretations, to be sure, but this is unavoidable: the computer can provide the numbers, but in the final analysis it is always the human observer who must draw the conclusions.

In the Taiwan project the general characteristics indicated a mean age of twenty-five (the professional engineer group had a mean of thirty-three), some 71 percent male overall (with the private language school group approaching equality with 44 percent female) overwhelmingly born in Taiwan (93 percent) and with their native language a Chinese dialect (99 percent) and of Chinese nationality (100 percent). Over 50 percent were Taiwanese, 31 percent from mainland families, and 8 percent Hakka (the private language school, however, had 44 percent of its students from mainland families).

The overwhelming number of students had studied English for more than seven years in public school (86 percent) and had largely limited further study to self-study programs of learning English (70 percent)—though 60 percent of the private school body indicated study in a private school (but it is uncertain whether that was inclusive or exclusive of the private language school, as the question was not clearly worded). Sixty percent of the population indicated that they also had contact with English in classwork where subjects were taught with English as the language of instruction, but only 15 percent overall indicated frequent contact with English speakers (but 39 percent for the private language school). The median age when English language study began was twelve to fourteen, the age of Junior Middle School where English language instruction is initiated on a mandatory basis in public schools.

In the students' evaluations of their English language study, there were mixed feelings. Only *some* value was given to classes in which the medium of instruction was English, though 87 percent of the students indicated they would take such a course. In factors that were regarded as most responsible for success in learning English, there was disagreement among the three sampled populations: (a) the university group largely attributed success to Middle School training, (b) the private language school gave more credit to their private language program, while (c) the professional engineer group attributed the bulk of their success to self-study. Little value was given to university instruction by any group (about 10 percent overall). On the question of the value of formal

English instruction in developing an adequate command of English, the usual answer was "little," and only about half of the subjects responded positively to the question whether or not the amount of English learned in middle or technical school was worth the effort. On the whole, the English language background of the subjects was not evaluated favorably.

On motivations for studying English, the vast majority indicated high interest from the time of their initial exposure to it in Junior Middle School, with increasing motivation thereafter as they became more aware of the potential value of English to their general studies and careers. The original motivation for studying English was largely the English language requirement, but this changed as time went on. Naturally, the most highly motivated subjects were generally those like the professional engineers in group (c) who planned to go to the United States in the near future. It is interesting to note in this respect the amount of time our subjects said they were willing to devote to the study of English. Nearly half of our sample were willing to devote one to three hours per day, and another quarter were willing to devote *more* than three hours per day to studying English.

In attitudes, it is interesting to note comparative evaluations of Chinese and English. Two-thirds of the sample believed that Chinese was better as a means of expression, but more than half still believed that English was more useful in work or study. The vast majority indicated that English gave them greater access to information in job or subject-matter areas of study, and most also believed English to be best for an international language. (But, significantly, nearly half still believed Chinese to be more useful in work or study, and 30 percent believed that Chinese would make the best international language.)

On questions relating to the value and relevance of English to students of science and technology, the answers were clear that the value is a considerable one. About 40 percent indicated that in professional or occupational matters they experienced daily difficulties due to a lack of adequate competence in English, and it was almost unanimously agreed that students of science and technology should study English, that English language study should be geared to occupational needs, and that chances of advancement in employment increase with a knowledge of English. The majority also felt that English was more important to students of science and technology than to students of other fields. This shows a clear conception of the professional and occupational value placed on English.

It is interesting to compare a series of questions on motivation with a series of questions on benefits derived from English. While only 25 percent of the overall sample indicated that English as a tool of study was the primary motivational factor, 60 percent indicated that educational benefits derived from their knowledge of English. In general, conversing with foreigners was a very low-valued factor, except among the private language group (35 percent), which contained a large number of business-oriented students who had daily contact with English-speaking customers or buyers.

The four language skills were ranked by nine different factors; the general order was: reading, listening, speaking, and writing. The greatest variability was in the position of speaking and writing, with writing being more important in some categories. In terms of frequency of use, listening rated higher than reading. In the case of desired command, however, speaking outweighed all other skills, indicating that speaking ability is desirable even when all other "objective" factors rate it very low.

Another set of questions dealt with registers and language skills. Generally, in speaking ability the highest ratings were given to the lowest-level tasks: giving routine instructions and for telephone conversations, rather than such things as giving oral reports, teaching in English, or giving public lectures. The same order held true for the equivalent listening tasks (listening to routine instructions, etc.). Reading and writing skills were a little more complex, with the same general direction from routine to complex tasks, but with a difference with regard to three hyperformal and formal tasks: for reading, texts and reference works scored the highest, followed by manuals, handbooks, technical reports, and the like—an effective reversal of the trend for speaking and listening. Likewise, in written materials, items such as outlines, summaries, lecture notes, and other formal writing skills ranked at the top of the list of tasks, but otherwise the progression was the same as for the speaking and listening skills. This indicates that reading and writing involved more extensive use of formal materials and skills than speaking and listening, where more casual usage is foremost in importance.

Attitudes toward the content and methods of English-language teaching indicated that the surveyed population wished the most emphasis to be placed on basic language skills (77 percent) rather than on educational and occupational needs (22 percent); however, we have already seen that the answers to other questions indicated that the value of English for educational or professional goals was very highly rated. (One question, for example, indicated that 86 percent of the surveyed population believed that English language instruction should be oriented toward occupational or educational areas.) The implication of this finding is that there is a need for a strong occupational and educational orientation in teaching materials in which the basic language skills are not neglected.

The dissatisfaction the surveyed population expressed with regard to their prior English-language training seemed to be largely related to the particular teaching methods that they had been exposed to. It appears that the three most frequent techniques used to teach English were reading essays, grammar rule learning, and translation, all of which were rated "not very successful." In the open-ended portion of our questionnaire, a strikingly large proportion of our sample also expressed the common view that the main shortcoming of the survey was that it seemed to overlook or downplay the importance of "methods of improving language teaching."

In terms of comparing attitudes toward the "difficult" aspects of English and the "valued" aspects of learning English, there is agreement on two of the three first-ranked items in both scales, with "sentence structure" and "vocabulary" high on both. But the first-ranked item in "difficulty" was "appropriate usage," which ranked next to last in terms of value. Also, pronunciation and spelling ranked as the two easiest aspects of learning English, but as high in rank in terms of value (second and fourth, respectively). Morphology or word formation ranked fourth in difficulty, but last in value. It must be emphasized that this is an area in which the surveyed populations had very little conscious, technical knowledge, and while it is interesting to note their evaluations for a number of pedagogical reasons, it is perhaps a less than proper basis for determining needs in terms of developing course designs for ESP.

In summary, perhaps it must be said that the surveyed population was fully aware of the importance of English in today's world and wished to have a working knowledge of it in professional and educational endeavors, with material oriented to these subjects where possible, but not at the expense of learning the basic language skills. The ranking of the four basic skills indicated that speaking was regarded as an important objective—despite the fact that it was ranked lowest in terms of need—a clear injunction to maintain a place for the spoken language even in technical fields. The ranking of tasks involved in daily use, insofar as it was investigated, indicated a general preference and need in terms of the most casual registers and the simplest tasks, except in the case of reading and writing, where technical skills in the formal area were most highly valued. These findings are by no means all obvious and it is unlikely that they could have been arrived at without the kind of information provided by the survey.

Critique of the Project. This phase is important if the survey is to be of much positive benefit to other investigators involved in similar projects in the future. The main defects that we have so far identified in the Taiwan project are the following:

(a) The questionnaire was fuzzy with regard to its objectives, as already noted. It was supposed to measure needs with reference to the ability of departments in Taiwan universities and colleges to offer service courses in EST; but it went far beyond this in scope, without a careful orientation provided by a clear set of theoretical or practical considerations.

(b) The questionnaire, as a result, did not delimit the parameters of the investigation carefully, but rather "scattered" the questions over a large and relatively uncontrolled area. It is valuable enough as a preliminary investigation, perhaps, but literally cries out for a more controlled follow-up study.

(c) The survey could also have been more selective with respect to the target population. The private language school was in many respects the most diverse, and also offered some of the most interesting results. As such, it did function as a kind of gauge against which to measure the specific needs in a technical college or university, but perhaps it introduced too large a number of irrelevant considerations into the study, as well. In addition, the theoretically most important subsample from the standpoint of the original goals of the project turned out to be the one that was the most poorly represented, i.e., the group of professional technicians and engineers.

(d) The survey was, of course, simply a measure of the subjective opinions of those surveyed, and did not involve the direct observation of actual uses or behaviors in the areas surveyed. Nor did it survey the attitudes of language teachers and other professional educators concerned with the matters at hand. Attitudes of students are interesting, but in many areas must be evaluated with care, realizing that the students' understanding of language (and even of the full nature of their proposed professional careers) is limited. Thus, a study should be balanced by other survey techniques, such as in-depth interviews and direct observation, to gauge more reliably the needs and expectations it reveals.

For all its faults, however, our study has apparently uncovered quite a number of interesting new facts, as well as suggesting some productive lines of inquiry not originally anticipated. Even more important, perhaps, is the opportunity it offers for subsequent investigators to learn from our missteps, as well as our achievements, toward the design and development of ESP programs, which will in time serve to satisfy the real requirements of the student populations for which they are intended.

3

An Analytic Approach
to Language Program Design

Lyle F. Bachman
University of Illinois
Urbana-Champaign

Gregory J. Strick
University of Illinois
Urbana-Champaign

Of the many language programs that fail to measure up to the original expectations of the people who plan, develop, and implement them, the majority, we believe fall short because of insufficient precision in the information the client and designer make available to each other and to themselves during the planning phase of the program. Frequently the client has only a very general notion of what learner outcomes he or she expects of the program. Regrettably, we, as language specialists, are often unresponsive to the client's lack of expertise in this area, and, rather than trying to elicit specific objectives from the client and guiding his or her priorities, we often design programs according to our own preconceived ideas of what a "reasonable" language program should include. Even when there is close client-designer contact during the pre-development phase, and even when objectives are clearly stated and jointly agreed to, the marketability of the program is often a matter of conjecture. That is, at this point neither the client nor the designer can determine very precisely what resources will be necessary to achieve the objectives they have set. Nor do they have a precise methodology for determining the optimum allocation of these resources. It is the purpose of this chapter to develop a model for the pre-development phase of language program design with which the language program designer can relate learning objectives directly to resource needs in a way that will enable him or her to determine what objectives are reasonable, given certain resources, or what resources are required by a given objective set. In order to illustrate how the model applies to actual programs, we have included a case study of a language program with which we have been directly involved.

LANGUAGE PROGRAM DESIGN MODEL

The model presented below has evolved from experience in numerous research and development projects and represents what has actually been tried out, at one time or another. Thus, although the theoretical aspects of the model may be interesting in their own right, our primary intention is to present what can actually be done—a set of operating procedures, if you will—in designing language programs. While we do not claim that the model will solve all of the designer's problems, there are several features we believe provide strong justification for its use. *First,* the model requires an accurate assessment of the client's needs and resources (or potential resources) in determining realistic program objectives. *Second,* it facilitates the establishment of clear program design alternatives, based on formulated objectives and available resources. *Third,* it enables the designer to determine the optimum program design, given specific resources and objectives. *Fourth,* it provides the means for a detailed specification of that optimum program design by the designer and client, in close collaboration. And finally, *fifth,* it establishes a framework for rigorous evaluation of the program during the development and implementation phases.

Much of what is incorporated into the design model presented here originates from the field of educational evaluation, which has had only limited application in the design of language programs to date. We believe it is fair to say that evaluation in language programs has focused primarily on the measurement of the individual student's acquisition of foreign language skills, on various factors such as intelligence, language aptitude, attitudes, and motivation, believed to affect the acquisition of language skills, or on issues of methodology. Examples are the Pennsylvania Language Project (Smith, 1970) and the GUME Project (Levin, 1971; Lindblad and Levin, 1970), both of which aimed at comparing the effectiveness of different methodologies in teaching foreign languages. In the St. Lambert Experiment (Lambert and Tucker, 1972), the research focus was on the interaction among student variables, particularly academic achievement and language proficiency, and the language use configuration of the learning environment. The evaluation of language programs themselves, however, is often an ex post facto activity, and, with a few notable exceptions, seldom is considered in language program design. Examples of language programs that are designed and developed for specific needs and that incorporate various features of the model we present below are the Hawaii English Program (State of Hawaii, Department of Education, 1972), aimed at developing an individualized English language arts program for students in the Hawaii public school system, and the Individualized Language Learning Project (Aiken and Bachman, 1977), aimed at developing an individualized EFL program for elementary school children in Thailand. This brief overview is not intended to show that language programs fail to incorporate evaluation considerations in the planning phase. However, it is our belief that an evaluation approach to language program design, particularly in EFL and ESP programs, is a fairly recent phenomenon, and that programs incorporating this approach are still the exception rather than the rule.

In contrast to EFL programs, evaluation has played a significant role in recent years in general curriculum development. Curricula in other subjects are commonly developed, tried out, evaluated, revised, retaught, and so on, until they have demonstrated their adequacy in meeting program objectives or their superiority over competing curricula (Portwood, 1976a). The model we are proposing incorporates several features of program evaluation as developed in the last ten to fifteen years. The notion of incorporating evaluation into program design from the beginning stages, as first elaborated by Cronbach (1963), has been further developed and refined by Scriven (1967, 1974), Stufflebeam (1971, 1974), and others. The salient features of program evaluation, as discussed by these writers, include (1) the assessment of needs, leading to (2) a clear statement of program objectives, in operational terms, (3) the consideration of the decision alternatives available to the program designer, (4) the trialling of the program, (5) the systematic monitoring of this try-out, through the collection of information, (6) the use of this information to relate observed outcomes to program processes, and (7) the making of decisions regarding the improvement of the program. Sanders and Cunningham (1973) have further distinguished "pre-development activities," which consist, essentially, of needs assessment and the evaluation of objectives. This comprises the first component of our model. Scriven, in his checklist for product evaluation (1974:12-22), includes the analysis of marketability:

1. Needs assessment (Justification)
2. Market (Disseminability)
3. Performance—True field trials
4. Performance—True consumer
5. Performance—Crucial comparisons
6. Performance—Long-term
7. Performance—Side effects
8. Performance—Process
9. Performance—Causation
10. Performance—Statistical significance
11. Performance—Educational significance
12. Costs and cost-effectiveness
13. Extended support

This is the second component of our model, and takes the form of resource assessment. The third component, mapping objectives onto resources, or the determination of achievable objectives within the limits of given resources, is from the field of econometrics (Wonnacott and Wonnacott, 1970; Casson, 1973).

Needs Assessment and Evaluation of Objectives

Any type of program development, whether completely original or an alteration of an existing program, must be justified, in terms of the needs it fulfills, to both the consumer and the supplier. A needs assessment is aimed at determining to what extent there is a genuine need or even a "defensible want," in Scriven's words, for the program being considered. As such, a needs assessment is quite distinct from a market survey. We all know that language programs are sellable; but so are pet rocks. In the majority of situations, it is the language program designer who is faced with the task of determining precisely what the needs of the program are. This task, essentially, involves determining the objective set for the program. In doing this, there are two primary considerations. First is the identification of clients. In the broadest sense, the clients are all those who will be affected by the program. This includes administrators, teachers, students, and, perhaps, interested parties in the university, corporation, or school system and in the community. In an ESP program for training helicopter pilots, for example, the clients may include, in addition to students, teachers, and administrators, pilot trainers, ground controllers, air traffic controllers, maintenance personnel, and many others whose interaction with the trainee pilot depends on the use of English. In an academic environment, the clients would certainly include professors who teach their courses in English, or who may require students to use English in reading course materials or writing reports. As we identify the clients we must also recognize and appreciate their limitations regarding the professional aspects of the program. Their training, experience, and talents, after all, lie in other fields, and just as we, as language teaching specialists, must realize our own naiveté in those fields, so must we realize that our clients are likely to be unfamiliar with the linguistic, psycholinguistic, and sociolinguistic factors involved in planning language programs. The second consideration is the framework for the needs assessment. It is essential that the objectives be stated, at this point, not in terms of processes or enabling objectives, but in terms of outcomes, or performance objectives. It obviously begs the question, for example, to indicate that one of the program's learning objectives is that students use the language laboratory. A more useful formula, for stating objectives, for both planning and evaluation, is, for example, "The student will be able to comprehend directions (to execute a given maneuver) when they are presented orally in English." Once clients have been identified and the objective framework clarified, the ideal procedure is then to elicit objectives from the clients. In most cases, however, it is the program designer who is placed in the position of preparing the objective set. Although this approach has obvious limitations in terms of the range of the objectives and biases of the designer, it is often the only practical way of getting the needs assessment initiated. Furthermore, an experienced program designer who carries out the next step, the evaluation of the objective set, can overcome many of these limitations.

In evaluating objectives, two types of analysis are available: logical and empirical (Stake, 1970). Since an objective is essentially a value or priority statement about a desired outcome, the first type of logical analysis is to determine the cogency of the argument behind each objective. An objective with no justifiable rationale can hardly be worth including. Second, it is important to consider the possible consequences of achieving a given objective. Program evaluations are all too full of unanticipated, undesirable side-effects associated with achieving various objectives. Many of these can be avoided by careful consideration and reformulation of objectives during the planning phase. A third type of logical analysis is to consider the objectives in relation to the broader goals of the system. If a given objective is at odds with the national language policy, for example, it obviously should be reconsidered.

In evaluating objectives empirically, it is strongly urged that, in addition to clients, language program specialists be consulted. Since several methods of empirical evaluation are available, we recommend the easiest, which is simply to ask for a ranking and weighting of the objectives, with specific instructions for how this is to be done. More difficult to construct, but sometimes more productive, methods include Lickert and semantic differential scales, as well as various sorting techniques. The end product of the needs assessment and evaluation of objectives is a list of performance objectives ranked and weighted in terms of importance or priority.

Resource Assessment

Often the designer plans a program on the basis of a thorough needs assessment and careful evaluation of objectives, but ignores the question of marketability; and consequently delivers to the client a program design that is essentially nonimplementable. A crucial question to be asked from the beginning stages, therefore, is, What factors will affect the implementability of the program? In answering this question, the first step is to conduct a thorough resource assessment. In the discussion below, we identify various resource factors we believe are relevant to language program implementability. We note, however, that the factors to be included in any given resource assessment will depend on the type of program envisaged. We believe there are three main factors to be considered in any resource assessment: physical (P); human (H); and cost (C). These three main factors can be represented in an equation defining the "Implementability Function" (I) of the resources, as follows:

$$I = P + H + C$$

Each of these main factors may be further specified. Physical factors, for example, may comprise Space (S), Materials (M_1), Method (M_2), Equipment (E), Laboratory (L), and Time (T), and may be specified as follows:

$$P = S + M_1 + M_2 + E + L + T$$

And again, each of the subfactors may be divided into finer specifications. Space, for example, might include classroom space, office space, work space, study space, and so forth. Materials may include basic student classroom materials, supplementary materials, teacher's guides, and other support materials. Method may be seen as the approach to a particular type of learning situation, including basic classroom management procedures, learning activities, the modification of materials, or a change of methodological emphasis. Equipment may include audio-visual aids, furniture, office equipment, materials production equipment, and so forth. We distinguish two types of Time: Development Time and Implementation Time. Both need to be considered in the resource assessment. Without defining these explicitly, it can be seen that the sequencing of these two types of Time will have an important effect on the Implementability Function. Typically, Development Time and Implementation Time are sequenced in three ways, as illustrated in Figure 3.1.

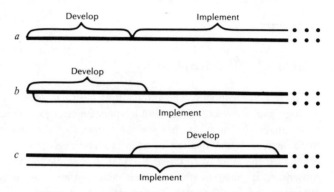

Figure 3.1 Development — implementation time sequences

Figure 3.1 a illustrates the ideal time line of a new program, in which development appropriately precedes implementation; b represents a more typical sequencing of a new program, in which there is little or no time for development before implementation; c represents the typical time line of an on-going program, where development (or redevelopment) may be started only after the existing program has proven inadequate, inappropriate, or both.

Just as the physical factor may be subfactored, the human factor may be seen to consist of teachers, administrators, learners, developers, supporters, and members of the given speech community. Each of these, in turn, is clearly complex. The teacher factor may include number, competence, motivation, attitudes, and so forth; likewise the learner factor. In the case of members, the speech community may constitute the academic or business community and the larger community of which it is a part. In both types of community, however, the functions of language use are an important human resource. That is, whether or not the use of the target language is reinforced within the speech community, through either actual community use of the target language or community approval of its use for some function, will affect the Implementability Function.

From this discussion, it can be seen that the specification of resources is hierarchical, as illustrated in Figure 3.2. At this point, an important consideration must be kept in mind: At no level are all of the factors

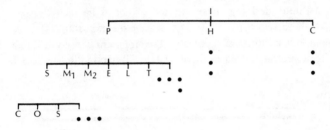

Figure 3.2 Resource hierarchy

completely independent. The interactions between materials and methodology and between teachers and learners are clear examples. The point to be made, however, is that *for the purpose of resource assessment,* some degree of specification is essential. The degree of specificity will depend on the amount of research evidence available to the designer, the consensus, if any, in the research and professional literature and, ultimately, on the professional judgment of the designer.

Having specified the factors of the Implementability Function, the program designer is then faced with the necessity of determining the relative importance of these factors for the program in question. That is, the factors and subfactors must be ranked and weighted in order of priority. Here, the first step is specifying the unit of assessment for each factor. It may be possible to assess some factors on the basis of an objectively quantifiable measure. A unit of space, for example, might be specified as one square (or cubic) meter. Learner language aptitude might be specifiable in terms of a test score. Other factors, such as the effect of the speech community, however, may have to be specified more subjectively. The next step is to assign a weight to each factor at each level, to indicate its relative importance. This process will necessarily be subjective, but should reflect the judgment of both the designer and the client as they collaborate in assessing the resources. The weighting will also reflect a particular program perspective, whether it be that of the "ideal" program, the desired program, or the minimum acceptable program. Whatever perspective is adopted, either explicitly or implicitly, it should be followed in weighting every factor.

The results of this process will be a series of equations, one at each level in the resource hierarchy, specifying the relative importance of the various factors in each. The Physical factor, for example, might be specified as follows:

$$P = 5S + 8M_1 + 10M_2 + 1E + 3L + 8T$$

This equation indicates that Method (M_2) is considered the most important factor, with a weight of 10, Materials (M_1) and Time (T) second, with weights of 8 each, and so on down to Equipment (E), with a weight of 1. We would point out that in addition to weighting, exponential or radical functions may be given to factors that are not linearly related to Implementability. Space and Time, for example, do not function linearly, since constant increments in Space or Time do not yield proportionate increments in Implementability. That is, there is a point at which increased Space or Time yield smaller and smaller benefits to the program. This can be accommodated in the equation by using the square of the values for these factors, as follows:

$$P = 5S^2 + 8M_1 + 10M_2 + 1E + 3L + 8T^2$$

In summary, then, the resource assessment consists of (1) identifying the factors and subfactors to be assessed, (2) specifying units of assessment for each, and (3) weighting each factor according to importance.

Resource-Objective Curves

The first two parts of the model, the needs assessment and evaluation of objectives and the resource assessment will, if done carefully, produce two scales, an objective scale and a resource scale, each consisting of factors ranked and weighted in order of importance or priority. Once this has been done, it would be useful if some objective method for relating these two scales were available. Such a technique can, in fact, be found in the determination of cost curves in econometrics.[1] In this procedure, we can relate two variables, in this case, resources and objectives, using the statistical method of multiple regression. To illustrate this procedure, we might specify the achievement of a given performance objective, say Reading Comprehension (RC), as a function of Materials (M_1) and Time (T), as follows:

$$RC = M_1 + T^2$$

By including actual values for these variables, such as reading comprehension achievement test scores, difficulty level of reading materials, and number of hours spent reading, we might find, for example, that it requires 100 hours of reading Level 3 difficulty materials (however that may be defined) to obtain a score of 80 percent on the XYZ reading test, while achieving a score of say 85 percent requires 150 hours and slightly more difficult materials. This relationship might be represented graphically as in Figure 3.3. Applying this procedure to the general problem of relating resources to objectives, we can, for example, determine the

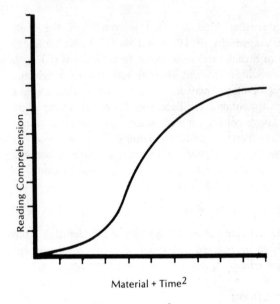

Material + Time^2

Figure 3.3 RC = M + T^2 curve

relationship between the Physical resource factor and a given objective level. Using the equation given above for Physical resources, we could specify the relationship between Reading Comprehension, say, and Physical resources as follows:

$$RC = 5S^2 + 8M_1 + 10M_2 + 1E + 3L + 8T^2$$

This equation will yield a curve we will call the "Optimum Physical Resource-Objective curve." Following the same procedure, we could also obtain an Optimum Human Resource-Objective curve. These two curves might take the shapes illustrated in Figure 3.4.

Using these Optimum Resource-Objective curves as parameters, it is now possible to match resources and objectives in a reasonably precise manner. One approach would be for the client and the designer to reach a decision regarding what they consider the Minimum Acceptable Program (MAP), in terms of the performance objectives on the objective scale. Suppose, for example, the Minimum Acceptable Program is one that achieves the first three performance objectives on the objective scale: perhaps these are objectives specifying certain reading skills. From the point on the objective scale that indicates the Minimum Acceptable Program, a horizontal line ("MAP line") is drawn, as illustrated in Figure

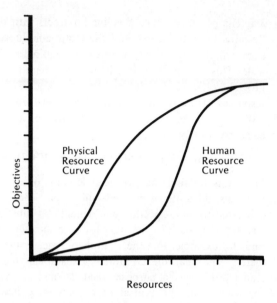

Figure 3.4   Physical and human resources — Objective Curves

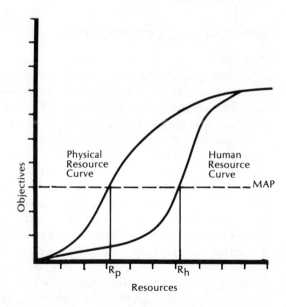

Figure 3.5   Determination of resources from MAP line

3.5. The points at which this line intersects with the Optimum Physical Resource-Objective curve and the Optimum Human Resource-Objective curve will determine the values of the required resources on the resource scale. This is illustrated in Figure 3.5, where the Minimum Acceptable Program requires 3 units of physical resources and 6 units of human resources. These values can then be transformed into actual physical resource requirements, for example, by solving for the factors in the equation given below:

$$3P = 3(5S^2 + 8M_1 + 10M_2 + 1E + 3L + 8T^2)$$

From this we find that we need 15 units of space, 24 units of reading materials, 30 units of method and so on. These units, in turn, can be converted to more specific requirements by substituting the appropriate assessment units into the next lower level resource equation. We might find, for example, that the 15 units of space transform into 2,500 square meters, and that the 25 units of materials transform into 6 general readers, 12 special-purpose readers, and a teacher's manual. This approach would be typical of a completely new program, where the allocation of resources should and often can be made on the basis of the program objectives.

APPLICATIONS OF THE MODEL

There are basically two types of program design situation to which the model applies: developing a completely new program and redeveloping an existing program. With a new program, the application of the model is reasonably straightforward. The designer, in close collaboration with the client, conducts the needs and resource assessments, projects the resource needs, and then presents the client with one or more decision options regarding the allocation of resources. How this presentation is actually carried out will depend upon the resource limitations, if any, on the given program and on the client-designer relationship. Our experience indicates that at this point the designer should be prepared to discuss several possible resource allocations in addition to the one he or she believes is optimum. These alternatives can be determined by considering the various possible resource allocations that could be made in order to achieve the minimum acceptable program objectives. If all goes smoothly, the designer and the client decide on a resource allocation that matches the program objectives, the resources are acquired and allocated, and program development begins. If, however, the resource needs exceed a given limit (most often budgetary), the designer and the client must reach a compromise decision, and in this situation the model can be used very effectively to demonstrate the consequences, in terms of program objectives, of a given reduction in resources. It is also often the case that resources are allocated before the designing of the program. In this situation the reverse procedure, mapping objectives from available resources, can be used to determine which objectives are achievable.

In redeveloping an existing program, the application of the model is more complex. This is because the number of decision alternatives will be larger and the process of deciding on any given change will be rendered more difficult because of the entrenchment of either the existing program objectives, the existing program resources, or both. In an existing program deemed inadequate for which the decision to redevelop has been made, essentially the same procedures are followed as in developing a new program. But changes in existing programs are not always initiated from concerns about output or performance. Legislatures and departments or ministries of education frequently allocate budgets that result in a net reduction in the availability of resources. In this situation the decision alternatives are clearly more complex. If the performance of the existing program is generally considered satisfactory, is it possible to reallocate resources and still meet the objectives of this program? If so, how? If not, what is the optimum resource allocation to achieve a more restricted set of objectives? What program objectives will have to be sacrificed? And are these sacrifices such as to render the program no longer acceptable? These and other questions can be approached in relatively precise manner by plotting program lines for the existing program, for the Minimum Acceptable Program, and for the program available with the projected resources, and then determining the various resource allocations required by these programs. An example of this situation is illustrated in Figure 3.6, where the existing program already has a surplus of resources, in terms of the objectives it is achieving, and there is a range of possible resource allocations that would enable the program to continue achieving its present objectives within the limits of the cut-back in allocated resources. Application of the model in cases such as this will clarify the decision alternatives and perhaps indicate a priority among these alternatives. Thus, while the choice, for example, between giving up a particular component or subset of a program and reducing the size of the program staff is never an easy one, the application of the model can provide the decision-maker with a principled basis for making such decisions and for justifying them.

These examples should make clear the range of program design situations to which the model can apply. They should also suggest how

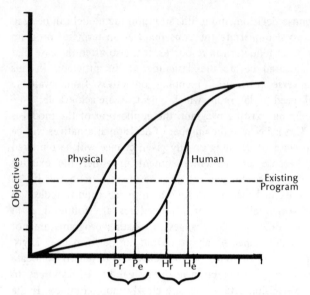

Figure 3.6   Differences in resource allocation between existing
(P_eH_e) and reduced (P_rH_r) resources

the model can be effectively employed by the program designer to
demonstrate to the client the relationship between resources and
objectives, and to enable the designer and client to more rationally reach
decisions regarding the "play-off" of resources against objectives, so that
the most effective program can be designed for a given set of needs and
objectives on the one hand and resources and limitations on the other.

CASE STUDY: A NEW LANGUAGE PROGRAM

This case study presents the initial phases of the development and
implementation of an English for Science and Technology (EST)
program at a newly inaugurated technological university in the Middle
East. The curriculum for the first two years consisted of a core program
in the sciences and included an English language program, the primary
objective of which was the development of competence in reading
English language textbooks and journals in the fields of science and
technology.

Needs assessment began from the perspective of the contractual
arrangements between the designer and the client (the university) and
proceeded informally through discussions with university administrators
and faculty, and specialists in the field of English language teaching.

Later, a formal needs assessment was conducted among the entire academic staff of the university. In the instrument, expressed needs were reformulated as performance objectives and were ranked in the order of priority. These were then weighted by the designer in consultation with university administrators and faculty. The weighting proved to be difficult in consultation. The administrators and faculty seldom considered objectives very specifically and preferred to delegate this responsibility to the designer.

In terms of general language skills, the order of priority that emerged from the needs assessment was reading, listening, writing, and speaking. Moreover, reading was determined to be twice as important as listening, which was twice as important as writing. Speaking was considered of minimal importance. Among the reading skills, reading textbooks was ranked first, reading journals second, and reading laboratory reports third. Among listening skills, listening to lectures had priority and among writing skills, writing notes on the lectures had priority. This ranking and weighting of objectives implied, as terminal objectives, that the students would be able to read English-language textbooks and journals in their fields, comprehend English-language lectures on their fields, take notes on the lectures, and ask for clarification of the lectures.

Since the university had been newly inaugurated, the resource assessment was conducted to determine the resources necessary to achieve the stated objectives. Accordingly, the physical and human resource factors were predicted and ranked, and then weighted by the designer in consultation with the university administration from the point of view of the desired program. Cost, the third resource factor, was reflected in the other two.

Among the Physical resources, Methodology and Time were ranked first, Materials second, Space third, and Equipment fourth. Moreover, Methodology and Time were weighted twice as important as Materials, which were weighted twice as important as Space, which was twice as important as Equipment, these five factors being the most relevant. Had a language laboratory been available at the outset of the program, it would have been weighted equivalently with Equipment. This procedure yielded the following specification for the Physical factor for M (Methodology), T (Time), B (Materials), S (Space), and E (Equipment):

$$P = 8M + 8T + 4B + 2S + 1E$$

Since the program was new, little data was available to facilitate establishing units of assessment for each of the above physical subfactors.

In order to project the Implementability Function for the subfactors onto the desired objectives, however, it was necessary to make some determination of the appropriate units for the allocation of resources. Therefore, the designer and client determined that there was sufficient classroom space for twelve classes of twenty-five to thirty students each, office space for every two instructors, space for a small library and conference and work space for both a materials development unit and a testing and evaluation unit. In addition, large lecture halls were available for examinations. Commercially available materials for developing reading skills were to be purchased in sufficient quantity for the first year's classes. Supplementary reading materials were limited, and listening comprehension materials were unavailable. The methodology of teaching reading skills was based on an initial assumption that competence in basic and subtechnical vocabulary and basic and technical sentence-level structure would enable the students to read scientific and technical texts. Exercises for the development of productive language skills were assumed to be necessary but not sufficient for the development of the receptive language skills. An electric typewriter was available, but there was no equipment for mimeographing materials. Other supplies, such as pens and paper, took a long time to obtain. A language laboratory was ordered, but was not available for the first year. Classes were scheduled for the morning hours, one hour per day, five days per week, for the first two years. Two hours of laboratory work per week were to be added to the schedule after the language laboratory had been installed. In addition to the class hours of English, the students were heavily loaded with class, laboratory, and workshop hours in chemistry, physics, mathematics, and design.

This process yielded basic units of assessment as follows:

Factor	1 unit equals—
Methodology (M)	5 lessons focusing on developing reading strategies
Time (T)	5 class hours (1 week)
Materials (B)	5 reading texts, each sufficient for 2 class hours
Space (S)	Sufficient space for approximately 15 students
Equipment (E)	1 typewriter

These physical resource factors would then need to be allocated to insure achievement of the highest priority program objective—reading.

The human resource factor was quite complex. Many of the subfactors overlapped and were interdependent. All of the teachers had English teaching experience with speakers of other languages and the majority held Master's degrees in TEFL or related fields. All were highly motivated and open to the culture of the students. The learners came to the university program with an average of six years of prior English instruction. An initial profile of the students' English proficiency was constructed on the basis of the English component of their university entrance examinations, their high school averages in English, and initial teacher observations. This profile indicated that approximately 40 percent of the students showed reasonable mastery of the criterion level set for the successful completion of high school English instruction, approximately 40 percent showed marginal mastery, and the remaining 20 percent were below criterion. The students were highly motivated to improve their reading proficiency in English. Administrators were convinced of the need for the students to have access to the scientific and technical information in English in their textbooks and journals. While these administrators comprised only a small portion of the faculty, they could strongly recommend a policy of English language use in subject area classes.

The community in which the university developed was in a very traditional provincial area of the country and the native language seldom gave up functions to the English language. Therefore there was virtually no reinforcement for English language use outside the academic community. On the other hand, the community contained a number of private or binational language institutes for instruction in the English language, so the need for the language was highly regarded. Nationally, there existed a slowly developing language policy toward the use of English for information access at the level of higher education, in the hope that the strong dependence on English-speaking expatriate professionals could be reduced.

Of the human resources, the teachers and learners were considered the two most important, because of their direct and continuous contact with the program. Less important were the administrators and their ability to institute a policy of English language use within the university community. Finally, the speech community itself was considered least important because of the relative isolation, in this case, of the university from the community.

The sequence of Development and Implementation Time imposed severe constraints on the designer, for little Development Time preceded the implementation of the program design. After a brief period of development, development and implementation proceeded simultaneously, which caused the projection of the resource factors onto the objective set and the prediction of necessary resources to fluctuate until the resources were actually utilized in the implementation.

At the beginning of the program there were no computing facilities, not even a programmable calculator; therefore no curve could be computed for the Implementability Function. However, the Minimum Acceptable Program line was easily set from the ranked objectives, and with the resources ranked and scaled, a close approximation of the appropriate resource allocation was determined.

With regard to setting the Minimum Acceptable Program line, the university administration decided initially that whatever objectives the designer considered essential should receive the appropriate allocation of resources. In this case, then, the program objectives were to be used to determine the program resources, rather than vice-versa. As utopian as this appears, the reality was that each university department had been given essentially the same assurance, and consequently maximized its efforts to obtain high priority resources to accomplish its high priority objectives. It soon became obvious that not all departments would be able to obtain their high priority resources because the total resources available were limited and had not been allocated. For example, there were only so many hours available in the mornings for university classes, and not every department could have all morning hours. Likewise, there were only a limited number of offices under construction, and not every department could be given the number needed. As the departments struggled to determine the availability of resources and secure those of highest priority, the English program negotiated away the lowest priority resources for higher priority ones in order to maintain the Minimum Acceptable Program line. When it became obvious that fewer resources were available or obtainable than were needed to achieve the Minimum Acceptable Program, the Minimum Acceptable Program line, unfortunately, had to be lowered.

The major limitations of the above model with respect to this case derived, from the nature of new programs in general, that little or no program data existed to realistically determine the resource curves, and, from the nature of this program in particular, that no means were available for reliably surveying resources. The model, nevertheless, provided the basis for initially setting the Minimum Acceptable Program line on the basis of a projection form resources to desired objectives and a prediction of necessary resources. A better informed initiation to program development and implementation could not have been made under the circumstances.

RESEARCH PROSPECTUS

The primary purpose of this discussion has been to describe and recommend a means for increasing the precision—in both procedure and content—with which language programs are planned and designed. We believe that the model we have described is applicable to any situation in which decision-makers (clients, designers, or both) are willing to make decisions (usually involving value judgments) regarding the relative importance of specific objectives and specific resources. The preciseness of these decisions and the accuracy of the predictions made from them depend on the preciseness with which the two scales, *objectives* and *resources,* are specified, and on the "validity" of the weights assigned to the factors on each scale. This suggests several lines for further research. First, although the methodology of needs assessment is well-developed, and a number of taxonomies have been proposed (Valette and Disick, 1969; Valette 1971; Moore and Kennedy, 1971), there are important questions still to be resolved regarding the specification of objectives. What degree of specificity is either necessary or desirable in stating objectives for program design? Are there any ordering relations among objectives, and if so, what is their nature? What sorts of hierarchical structures, if any, obtain among objectives and subobjectives? The development of needs assessment instruments based on detailed taxonomies of language skills would be one approach to answering some of these questions. Particularly promising, in this regard, is the research in needs specification and instrumentation being conducted by John Munby (1977, 1978). The assessment of resources is even less developed and, perhaps, more problematical. One approach that suggests itself is that adopted by Hayes, Lambert, and Tucker in the development of a process study checklist of language teaching principles and procedures (Hayes, Lambert, and Tucker, 1967). Following this approach, lists of resource factors could be elicited from ESL/EFL specialists, program designers, and, perhaps, clients. These factors could then be rated, in a number of ways, by a selected judgment group according to their importance (or nonimportance) to either ESL/EFL programs in general or to various types of specialized programs. The third line of research is simply the application of the procedures outlined in this paper to the planning and design of specific language programs. It is this sort of research which, although perhaps less appealing because of its "action" setting and impurity of design, we believe will ultimately produce the most valuable insights into the problem of language program design.

NOTE

1. Portwood (1976b) uses curves of constant cost and constant expected educational benefit to determine an optimal curriculum development design, in an approach that is similar, in several respects, to that presented here.

4

Register Research Design*

Joe D. Palmer
Concordia University
Montreal, Quebec

In this chapter I make several observations on the topic of *register,* defining the term and placing it in the center of the concern about the uses of language. I assert that register is a norm of language use, or a field of discourse, which is essential to a discussion of style; style being defined as the aggregate of linguistic markers that show a statistical trend in relation to the norm or register under consideration. Style is seen as a subvariety of register, not as a set of peculiarities in relation to the whole language.

I then comment on studies of linguistic units that have been quantified in order to characterize specific registers for the task of designing courses in English for Specific Purposes, pointing out that the use of authentic resource materials may make such analyses and such syllabuses unnecessary.

In conclusion, I make the point that cohesion devices, being macrolinguistic units, are different in kind from sentential grammatical categories and lexical items. It is doubtful whether any quantification of

*An earlier version of this chapter appeared in the *Proceedings* of the Fifth AILA Congress (Association International de Linguistique Appliquee), held in Montreal, August, 1978.

cohesion devices will prove useful to language course planners and students of style in the way that the specification of the relative frequency of occurrence of grammatical and lexical items has done so far.

REGISTER AND STYLE

Language teachers, whether they are dealing with native or nonnative speakers and readers, are faced with the problem of getting their students to comprehend fully what they read. Those who teach literature are very much aware of the lack of appreciation of style on the part of native readers. It is of course the students' lack of familiarity with the contextually related norms (or registers) of the language that causes them to be unaware of the subtleties, or even of the gross markers, of style.

As an example of a register and of a style (which I will not attempt to analyze here) the following dialogue from a novel will serve. The register might be called a "man-to-man talk" since it involves two lone, mature men who have been in love with the same woman. The style is unmistakably that of a popular American writer. It might be character- ized as tough talk.

> "You know what I'm going to do?"
> "No."
> "I'm going to head north right out of this swamp. I'm going to drive straight to Virginia, up the Shenandoah Valley, and pick up Frances, who has a horse farm near Lexington. I'll say to her: Let's go back to Tanzania. We were there once. We lived in a Land Rover. We saw leopard. She's a soldier, a good girl. She might even—She's always been my love. I took her once to Spain and showed her the Ebro River, where I fought. Yes, Christ, I did that too. Can you believe it? She's a good girl, a comrade. She's a comrade, brother, daughter, lover to me. All I have to do is say, Honey, let's go back to the high country, and she'll go. Jesus what an idea you've given me! I might even do a film. What do you think of a film about a man and a woman who are good comrades, go on a hunt, and then have good sex together?"
> "It sounds fine."
> (Walker Percy, *Lancelot,* p. 217. Reprinted with permission of Farrar, Straus and Giroux, Inc.)

We would be unable to appreciate the style markers that distinguish this selection were it not for the context of situation, and the contextually related norm, that is, the register that language users implicitly understand because of their prior experience with the language. Those who recognize the parody of Hemingway's style in the selection know the register extremely well. They have experienced similar language situations, and so they are able to contextualize the text at hand without hestitation. They have shared enough language experiences with others to know immediately enough about a discourse to understand and appreciate it. In short, being able to contextualize a discourse depends upon the many modalities of experience. I would like to suggest that a study of social phenomenology, of the task of relating one's experience of others' behavior, to others' experience of one's behavior (Laing, 1973), would help both literary critics and language teachers do a better job. The inner and outer worlds of our experience are both equally real. Experience is an often invisible yet formal way of knowing, of which language is a part. It is abstract and culturally determined just like language. Experience is the stuff of situations. Situations inform meaning through the inter-level of context. The context of situation is basic to a description or definition of register.

As far as I know there does not yet exist any operational taxonomy for texts along this dimension we are calling register. Most studies of register have avoided social function by labelling texts in general ways, without showing what detailed purposes they exist for (Palmer and Mackay, 1978). I would like to suggest that more precise descriptions of registers can be made by considering the several functions of any discourse.

In his essay "On Defining Style" in Spencer's *Linguistics and Style* (1964), Nils Enkvist claims that style is the occurrence of style markers which stand out from a contextually related norm. He defines style in such a way as to suggest that style and register are intimately related. Although his use of the term *register* is quite limited, the concept of register is essential to his thinking. In his conclusion he urges further study in the classification of contexts (that is, in the description of registers), observing that even though it may be impossible to achieve exacting scientific rigor in the classification of contexts—

> We should keep in mind the fact that people use language for "social purposes in a socio-physical environment." This socio-physical context must be admitted at all levels of linguistic analysis. If not, we risk ignoring the most important fact of language in use. (Enkvist, 1964)

The sociophysical context is in effect the major determinant of register. As Catford (1965) once defined it, register is the subvariety of dialect that correlates with the social roles being played by the performers. Thus we make use of different registers appropriate to the several roles we play, such as husband, mother, adviser, professor, secretary, and so on. Social role, however, becomes somewhat abstracted as a determinant of register when the register is in the written medium. In written language the rhetorical purpose—the use to which the language is being put, or the field of discourse—may through convention become the major determinant.

A further view of register includes, in addition to social roles and rhetorical purposes, the aspects of the code that relate to the functions of language. If a discourse emphasizes or is focused upon the person speaking or writing, its function is affective, emotive, and expressive; if the discourse is directed at the addressee, its function is to show purposeful advice, commands, and directions (conative); if the discourse emphasizes the message, its function is poetic; if it emphasizes human contact, its function is interaction management (phatic); if it emphasizes the code, then its function concerns the language itself (metalinguistic) (Jacobson, 1960). However, if the discourse has to do with that which lies outside interpersonal and textual concerns, that is, if it emphasizes the larger sociophysical context, then its function is denotive, cognitive, and referential (see Chapter 5). Its function is in a sense what Halliday (1973) calls the ideational macrofunction . It is perhaps this referential contextual function that is of the greatest concern to language course planners who intend to analyze registers.

In regard to style, it seems reasonable to regard a style as a subvariety of a register, analogous to an ideolect being a subvariety of a dialect. The phenomenon of style depends upon the expectation that certain forms are apt to occur in certain contexts. Without matching a text against a contextually related norm, consciously or unconsciously, we can have no perception of style.

QUANTIFYING LINGUISTIC UNITS

Before going on to report on two studies of registers which were used to inform the preparation of materials for teaching English for Specific Purposes, I would point out that there is a fundamental question about the use of inauthentic teaching materials. The analysis of registers is beside the point if authentic resource materials are used instead of cooked-up materials. Even the most carefully prepared and fully informed materials based on the analysis of target discourse still remain to some degree artificial. This artificiality, when added to the entire set of tricks we are calling classroom language, makes classroom discourse appreciably different from the target discourse that students need and want. If we are to close the gap between classroom and target discourse, perhaps only authentic resource materials should be used. (Phillips and Shettlesworth, 1978. See Phillips's discussion of this question in Chapter 6.)

McTear (1975) points out that EFL classroom language is very complex and different from target discourse. In the classroom the language is concentrated upon functions that differ from many of the target discourse functions. In particular, the metalinguistic, pedagogical, and personal functions come to the fore. Much classroom discourse has to do with the form of the language, the content of some subject that the resource materials are about, and the personal interaction of the addressers and the addressees, and their phatic concerns. Since these kinds of discourse are often different from what the student needs to command, say, to become a successful civil engineer, we may suppose that success with classroom language does not ensure success with target discourse.

Whether or not to analyze registers becomes a matter of the possibility of adjusting the available methodologies and academic situations. For example, if the teachers are incapable of teaching authentic materials, which is often the case, it would seem preferable to design good but inauthentic materials that are teachable.

However, Coulthard (1977) observes that even the most carefully prepared materials that include all the lexical and grammatical features of the target discourse lack communicative value. The many new textbook series in English for Science and Technology are merely texts rather than discourses, even though written discourse types such as classification, explanation, definition, generalization, etc., and logical operations such as induction and deduction are practiced through them. Their faults stem from their lack of authenticity. Their scientific content is frequently suspect and many passages are not grammatically or rhetorically acceptable.

These objections aside, however, one of the most interesting examinations of registers in recent literature is Rosaline K. Chiu's "Measuring Register Characteristics: A Prerequisite for Preparing Advanced Level TESOL Programs" (1975), which, after rather exhaustive definition of register and discourse, presents the results of her study of the language used in administrative correspondence and boardroom discussions. Chiu's study is based on two very straightforward techniques: a vocabulary count of lexical verbs, and a statistical comparison of formatives of the auxiliary in formal and informal speech and in writing.

Chiu defines register as "varieties of a language according to use." That is, "register characteristics are sets of linguistic forms found to have a regular connection with a particular use of the language in a particular situation, or sets of situations," a definition deriving from Halliday, McIntosh, and Strevens (1964).

Register is said to vary in three ways, according to the (1) field, (2) mode, and (3) manner (tenor) of discourse.

1. Field: Rhetorical purpose
2. Mode: Medium, spoken or written
3. Manner: Social role and attitude (style)

The field of discourse is further divided into technical and nontechnical areas. Technical fields are progressively narrowed by disciplinary topics, such as legal, medical, chemical, business, etc., and then further characterized as to semantic categories such as authorizing, informing, requesting, and sending.

Chiu argues that measured register characteristics should be considered necessary for materials preparation for advanced level ESL students. She maintains that this information is essential for the selection, gradation, and presentation of particular registers according to the learner's needs. This argument handily rests on the need to serve the learner's motivation in order to secure results, and is disputable only insofar as the reification of language for teaching purposes is disputable.

Chiu found that in the administrative correspondence she analyzed certain verbs were used more frequently than in the texts analyzed for the preparation of lists such as West's *General Service List of English Words* (Longman, 1936). Comparing the high-frequency verbs of administrative correspondence with the verbs of the Kuchera and Francis, *Computational Analysis of Present-Day American English* (Brown University Press, 1967), which analyzed about 1,000,000 words of texts, she found that these verbs had lower frequency. (See Table 4.1.)

Table 4.1 Chiu's comparison of high-frequency verbs in administrative correspondence

	Chiu	*Kuchera*
ATTACH	187	44
ENCLOSE	164	13
APPRECIATE	148	39
REFER	129	108
FORWARD	123	119
REQUEST	118	83
ADVISE	113	48
THANK	83	82

Her conclusion is that it is possible to work out an inventory of frequent and thus necessary lexical items, for purposes of teaching the use of this register of English.

Chiu analyzed the verb phrases in her corpus (8,289 items) in terms of the formatives that were present. That is, verb phrases were counted according to whether the verbs were present or past, whether they contained modals, passive voice, the perfect, or the progressive. It is interesting to note the different proportions of these formatives in the three registers (see Table 4.2). In particular the complexity of written language is shown through the increased incidence of mood and voice and the decrease in the number of simple tense forms when speech and writing are compared.

Table 4.2 Chiu's comparison of frequency of formatives in three registers

Verb Phrase	Informal Spoken	Formal Spoken	Administrative Writing
Unmarked (Simple present)	57.8%	54.0%	32.1%
Marked in tense only (Simple past)	29.1	27.0	10.0
Marked in mood (Modal)	40.4	34.4	44.2
Marked in voice (Passive)	9.9	12.0	47.3
Marked in phase (Perfect)	11.0	18.7	14.9
Marked in aspect (Progressive)	13.9	13.7	7.5

Another study, by Ronald V. White (1974), maintains that many TESL courses miss the mark because course planners have neglected to study the frequency of occurrence of grammatical items. Contrary to popular assumptions, he found that simple verb forms exceed complex ones in frequency of occurrence, and that in a special register (scientific reportage) a high incidence of passive voice is normal (nearly two-thirds of the verb groups counted). This register, scientific reportage, is defined as follows:

FIELDS: (i) Narration of sequence of processes already completed
       (ii) Description of results
       (iii) Interpretation of results
MODE: Written, to be read silently
TENOR: Formal, impersonal, objective
PROVINCE: Specialist, technical

But in "scientific description" (general trends, procedures, and principles) where the writer is an instructor and not a reporter, the balance of verb group factors changes; the passive drops to below 25 percent, simple verb groups constitute two-thirds of the total.

To counter the notion that specifying registers as, say, that of traffic policemen or hairdressers, is a trivialization of the concept, he suggests that register variation is a function of "communicative function or role of the user," i.e., in field.

What White is saying is that processes like exemplification, causality, comparison, contrast, analogy, etc., are the variables that cause grammatical differences. It is the field that determines the frequency of occurrence of grammatical patterns. Field of discourse or expository technique refers to the reason why a writer is using language: in order to persuade, to convince, to lie, to explain, and so on.

Further specific results of White's study include the observation that complex prenominal expressions [Those first three fine old stone French architect's houses . . .] "are vitually unheard of in actual language use." In a strong statement concerning the theoretical misdirection of recent TGG-informed materials, White denies that the passive is merely a manipulation of the active voice. He furthermore points out that a student may need to read descriptions, but he or she may also need to write reportage, and that these fields differ. In his conclusion he maintains that detailed discourse analysis must include an account of cohesion, and a study of how conceptual categories or expository techniques are manifested in lexico-grammatical units.

In a workshop at Chulalongkorn University in Bangkok in May, 1975, my colleagues and I found by comparing three university-level texts (Mahan's *University Chemistry,* Samuelson's *Economics,* and Kneller's *Foundations of Education*) that the chemistry text contained nearly twice as many subordinate clauses, relative to the number of main clauses, as did the other two texts, that the education text used vocabulary repetition three times more frequently than did the economics text, and that the chemistry text used more than twice as many sentence connectors as the economics text. Economics and chemistry used three times the number of comparatives as education but education used three times as many deictic expressions as economics (Palmer, 1977). Whether these differences have to do with register or with style remains a question that deserves an answer.

It is possible to regard teaching materials based on the analysis of register as a positive step forward if they are presented in situations that replicate authentic target discoursal opportunities. And there is the rub and the challenge to the language-teaching profession (see Chapter 6).

COHESION AND COHERENCE

Cohesion is well-enough known for me not to go into a description of it here (see Halliday and Hasan, 1976). I must say that in no instance have my students been able to show that cohesion devices correlate with anything useful to language program planners. This is not to say that the quanitification of cohesion devices will not eventually be found useful in characterizing a particular register. On the other hand, there *is* reason to think that cohesion will show correlations with the language of social stratification. Singh and Stanton (1978) purport to show that the distribution of cohesion devices in discourses by sixteen young adult native-speakers of Quebec French correlates with the three socio-economic groups that they represent. Interestingly, my students have found no real distributional differences among the cohesion devices in the three stylistically distinct parts of Hemingway's tour de force, "A Natural History of the Dead." Nonetheless, allow me to state that I am certain that a knowledge of the nature of cohesion devices is absolutely essential to every language teacher, particularly to those concerned with teaching people to read.

At this point, permit me an aside for the record. Halliday and Hasan say that conjunctive elements, that is, sentence connectors, are not cohesive in themselves because they are not co-referential. They do not reach out into the text. They do not work on the lexical and grammatical levels even though they presuppose other components in the discourse. Unfortunately, some studies of cohesion confuse sentence connectors with cohesion devices.

While the study of cohesion provides interesting lexical and grammatical insights into the structure of text and the nature of register, the possibility of finding linguistic correlates to some rhetorical principles is a very exciting prospect. Discourse analysis promises some insights into the nature of rhetorical coherence. Texts are both cohesive and coherent, coherence being given by the appropriate use and sequencing of rhetorical devices.

In spite of Halliday and Hasan's caveat that—

> it is doubtful whether it is possible to demonstrate generalized structural relationships into which sentences enter as the realization of functions in some higher unit, as can be done for all units below the sentence,

text is surely an exponent of discourse just as clauses are exponents of propositions, and grammatical functions are exponents of concepts and notions (see Hymes, 1972; Sinclair and Coulthard, 1975; Spencer and Gregory, 1964; Hendricks, 1976; and Gutwinski, 1976).

Ongoing research into rhetoric and style is providing greater understanding of the semantic stratum that overlies syntax and cohesion (see Smalley, 1977). Our understanding the nature of register requires, in addition to lexical and grammatical data, information from studies of cohesion and coherence. Only then will we be able to make an operational taxonomy for the classification of texts that takes both the syntactic and semantic levels of language into account. Such studies await the development of the field of discourse analysis, the topic of the next chapter in this book.

5

Discourse Analysis

Joe D. Palmer
Concordia University
Montreal, Quebec

It is not easy to find one's way around in the field of discourse analysis. Trying to do so is a painful and frustrating business. Although discourse analysis is a rich field for the researcher, it is a nightmare for the ESP course planner looking for an ordered set of descriptive techniques or rational explanations.

In this chapter we try to separate out textual analysis from discourse analysis as two different but complementary ways of looking at language in use, and then move to a consideration of some of the current endeavors in semantics, stylistics, sociology, psychology, and linguistics that have a bearing on the problem.

More specifically, we pay attention to how Jacobson's aspects and functions might be related to Halliday's macrofunctions and Austin's performatives. This presentation is something like an aerial photograph taken from a great height. The details are blurred but the general topography is clear.

Implicit in much recent writing on discourse analysis is the supposition that there is a relation between text and situation substance that obtains through some sort of mediating level. It is assumed by most writers on the subject that text is an exponent of discourse just as clauses are exponents of propositions, and just as grammatical functions (subjects, objects, verbs, etc.) are exponents of notions or concepts (Gutwinski, 1976; Hendricks, 1976; Spencer and Gregory, 1964; Sinclair and Coulthard, 1975; Hymes, 1972).

All other units of analysis that are ranked below discourse in a hierarchy, which includes pragmatic speech acts, propositions, and concepts, are exponents of discourse. Using the terminology of stratificational grammar, we may say that this lowest level of concepts or functions is the base of the semantic stratum that overlies text and syntax. It is not at all clear how these ranks are to be described. While it is intuitively obvious that the semantic stratum does have structure, current endeavors do not yet show how this structure can best be exposed. It could be that discourse is an open-ended string of performatives that links predicates and their variables to the context of situation. The structure of a paragraph or of a dialogue is conceived on the semantic level (Gutwinski, 1976), but the question of how to describe this level as an ordered arrangement of items or as a hierarchy of rank-scale units remains an intellectual bramble bush.

We might define a discourse as a connected and self-contained body of language that has some identifiable instrumental or integrative purpose. Intuitively we feel that certain pieces of language have noticeable boundaries. It even appears that some stretches of language, particularly those of ritual use, are culture bound. This is to say that dialogues appear to be largely predetermined by learned expectations in that it is generally accepted that much of our language behavior involves social control (Abercrombie, 1956). On one level, written discourses are somewhat easy to characterize. Such obvious discourse types as definition, explanation, exemplification, conclusion, cause and effect, chronological procedures, classifying, etc., are relatively simple to identify because of the perceptively logical form of edited expository writing. Most American composition manuals draw upon this level of characterization (e.g., McCrimmon, 1976; Brooks and Warren, 1970). Recent attempts to characterize the language of various specialisms for ESL learners, with strong theoretical bases, are those by Allen and Widdowson (1978) and Bates and Dudley-Evans (1976). These applied linguists distinguish between the grammatical properties of language on the one hand, which are concerned with the mechanics of text (how the formal devices of syntax and lexis are used to combine words into sentences and sentences into continuous prose), and with the communicative value of the prose on the other. The latter recognize how sentences are used to perform acts of communication in scientific fields and what combinations of these acts are most characteristic of various specializations.

The selection of the linguistic content of a program to be used to teach a language for a special purpose depends heavily upon adequate and, equally important, appropriate descriptions of the language associated with the specialism in question. An appropriate description will be one that describes not only the syntactic features of the language but also the communicative features.

In "Teaching the Communicative Use of English" we learn that what is needed is—

> a shift of the focus of attention from the grammatical to the communicative properties of the language. We take the view that the difficulties which the students encounter arise not so much from a defective knowledge of the system of English, but from an unfamiliarity with the English use [N.B.: not "usage"] .... (Allen and Widdowson, 1978:58)

It is in the mastery of the production and comprehension of communicative acts that are related to uses for which the learner needs and wants to employ English that the key to effective learning lies. However, there does not yet exist any communicative syllabus based on an analysis of the appropriate discourses (Coulthard, 1977). At first glance, the new series of textbooks for EST seem to offer students of science and technology an innovative course in communicative acts. Although written discourse types are frequently presented (classification, definition, generalization, and explanation) and logical operations such as induction and deduction are practiced, the passages in these series, according to Coulthard, are actually *text* rather than *discourse* (Coulthard, 1977). As Coulthard says,

> In fact the books are, in some respects, a more subtle version of the earlier, ridiculed mistake:
> Where is the typewriter?
> The typewriter is in the cupboard. (Coulthard, 1977:153)

Coulthard's reservations about the presentation of discourse in these series stem from their alleged lack of authenticity. He notes that their scientific content is often specious and that many passages are not acceptable English.

In reaction to reductionist experience with linguistics it might be helpful to make a more expansionist point of view of language and concentrate attention on the uses we put it to: Discourse is the *communicative* functions of a text expressed in units higher than the sentence; e.g., in paragraphs and episodes.

A text is both coherent and cohesive. Coherence is given by the appropriate use and sequencing of rhetorical devices. Cohesion is a function of grammar and lexicon. But discourses do not have the sort of structure that sentences have. Discourses are organized according to principles of rhetoric which may be seen as those uses of language that provide unity, coherence, and emphasis (Marder, 1960), or as techniques of exposition and inquiry such as observation, description, analysis, comparison, contrast, analogy, illustration, prediction, and so on (Horn, 1971; Mackay and Mountford, 1976; Strevens, 1971), or as implicit presuppositional information (Selinker, Trimble, and Trimble, 1976).

Traditional school rhetoric no doubt contains many keys to the structure of discourse. The concepts of rhetoric belong to a venerable tradition that goes back beyond the medieval concern with the trivium, that group of studies consisting of grammar, rhetoric, and logic. Indeed, a synonym of rhetoric is *discourse*. There is a mysterious bond that links pieces of language to our ideas, and this bond or relation in turn leads "to the miracle by which ideas pass from one mind to another" (Barzun and Graff, 1957). The linguistic expression of a proposition "combines a subject of discourse with a statement in regard to this subject" (Sapir, 1921). Discourse is explained in school rhetoric as the manipulation of language to achieve certain desirable qualities such as unity, coherence, emphasis, variety, order, development, coordination, subordination, paraphrase, point-of-view, tone, and attitude (Williams, 1973). An understanding of these manipulations depends upon the reader or writer's familiarity with the special uses of the language that require these rhetorical devices to be employed.

Recent attempts to focus attention on notions, concepts, and ideas as they reflect communicative competence come under the general term, *The Semantic Approach*. The Semantic Approach to language teaching is a step forward from the syntax-based syllabuses. Concentrating on what people want to do with language is preferable to unapplied presentation of the code alone. Nevertheless, concepts and functions by themselves are not sufficient to explain communication. It is the organization of phonology, graphology, lexis, grammar, and notions in discourse that allows communication to take place in either direct or indirect interaction (Widdowson, 1977). Discourse is compounded of meaningful elements of a notional inventory. But these concepts have no more utility than do kernel sentences until they are related by the user to contexts by means of discourse. Real communication is complex. Readers and listeners have the task of understanding whatever is written and said according to their own attitudes, beliefs, interests, and intentions, and their previous experience, and knowledge of the language, and the conventions governing its communicative use. The organizing principle or framework of discourse is not a static series of acts of communication that can be discovered by operating upon texts in order to describe rule-governed patterns (Widdowson, 1975). There are no rewrite rules for discourse. Interpreters who understand connected pieces of language must do so by creating personal meaning for themselves.

Thus a psychological investigation is necessary to discover the ways in which discourse works. After all, understanding and composing language are ongoing accomplishments. The ability to do is peculiar to each individual. Language use is a creative activity, a matter of interpretation of all the factors involved in the situation. Given the elusiveness of exact meanings, the importance of personal involvement, and the fact that the learner's cognitive map changes as he or she predicts and hypothesizes (Widdowson, 1975), it is no wonder that we cannot profitably begin with text as the unit to analyze. Widdowson maintains that meanings are derived from discourse by a process of practical reasoning; they are created, not discovered. Reading or continuous listening is interaction through a text. It depends upon a general yet selective discourse that addressees derive from text by pretending (perhaps unconsciously) that they are engaged in a reciprocal dialogue between themselves and the text. Dakin illustrates this interactional relationship very well in his "Lecture on Linguistics" in which he suggests how the readers or listeners negotiate meaning from a piece of discourse (Dakin, 1973). They hold in their minds a sort of dialogue in which the addresser and addressee roles of dialogue are reconstituted. In this reconstitution of an imagined dialogue the processes of interaction relate the affective and cognitive messages of the text to the knowledge and experience of the reader. Thus reading is not essentially different from conversation. Coulthard speculates that full stops (periods) are interaction points—

> places where the writer thinks the reader needs to stop and ask questions about the previous sentence, questions whose range [the writer] initially [restricts] by the structuring of [his or her] argument and which [he or she] subsequently [answers] in the next or later sentences. . . . (Coulthard, 1977:181

In their concern with discourse analysis, applied linguists engaged in LSP work have more in common with literary critics than with orthodox linguists (Widdowson, 1975b). LSP and stylistics are concerned with both noting and describing the variation that exists in language and specifying the extent to which varieties differ from one another in systematic as opposed to random ways. In addition to a traditional concern with the *form* of language, each is concerned with matters regarded by the orthodox linguist as extra-linguistic, that is, by factors external to the code itself. The traditional categories of linguistic analysis are capable of handling *only a part* of language as seen in these broad terms.

The notion of context of situation as employed by Firth (1957) is a useful starting point for the discourse analyst:

1. The relevant features of participants (persons, personalities)
   (a) The verbal action of the participants
   (b) The nonverbal action of the participants
2. The relevant objects
3. The effect of the verbal action

Context of situation is a useful abstraction at the most gross level of analysis. Defining the context of situation yields the register of the text under scrutiny. The succeeding steps taken to characterize, analyze, and describe the data will depend very much on the purposes of the researcher. The literary critic may be satisfied with broad categorizations such as narration, description, elegy, and so on. The applied linguist concerned with the creation of LSP programs will be interested in units of analysis that eventually can be translated into instructional units, for his or her principal concern is not in the characterization of the data as an end in itself but as a means for its mastery in either receptive or productive terms. In other words, the applied linguist's analysis of discourse will depend upon *what kind of a system* he or she believes language to be, how he or she believes it can most easily be *learned,* and the most appropriate way it might be *taught.*

The LSP program planner on the one hand may be interested in the detailed interaction between doctor and patient, lawyer and client, executive and secretary, pilot and air-traffic controller. On the other hand, he or she may be interested in the choices available to a scientist wishing to communicate the results of an experiment to fellow researchers through the pages of an appropriate journal. In all cases, he or she is likely to be concerned with the most appropriate and effective means of presenting this information to a learner so that the latter may master those aspects of the entire system that are available for his or her purpose. Nonetheless, he or she must begin with a consideration of register that depends on the context of situation. Language is not monolithic. The concept of register is based on this assertion (Ure, 1969; Palmer, 1977). Ure (1969) uses three dimensions for the classification of register types: (1) medium, (2) social function, and (3) formal code characteristics.

This classification system allows different kinds of texts to be labelled, but it allows for a more delicate breakdown *only* along the dimension of formal syntactic and lexical features. In other words, once the spoken/written distinction has been made and the social function determined in terms of the extent of involvement, the only detailed specifications of difference that can be expanded upon are those at the phonological, syntactic, and lexical levels. Despite the fact that Ure *does* take into consideration social function, she does not provide an operational taxonomy for the classification of texts along this dimension. Hence, most studies of register have glossed over social function in the most general way, labelling the registers, for example: the language of government administration, the language of academic study, or the language of science.

In their search for a framework within which the external sources of variation might be handled systematically, both sociological and philosophical concepts have been used (Firth, 1957; Halliday, 1973; Crystal and Davy, 1969; Gregory, 1967). In the United States, the ethnolinguists were tackling a similar problem although from a different starting point. They began with the social functions and moved toward determining the forms predominantly chosen, in specified contexts, for their realization in language (Hymes, 1972; Gumperz, 1972; Sacks, 1972; Schegloff, 1968). Moreover, in most cases they were interested in dyadic interaction as opposed to one-source communications such as written texts or formal speeches and lectures. Further applicable knowledge may come from the folklorists and the French anthropological structuralists.

The complex problem at the very center of any approach to analyzing discourse or providing a model for the analysis of discourse is of a dual nature. First, there is the difficulty of exhaustively specifying the functions that can be or are realized through language, and second, there is the inevitably subjective element in assigning any stretch of text to one or another of the functional categories set up.

Hornby (1954) was aware of the need for the functions performed by given formal items to be associated with the teaching of these items. In Section V of his *Guide to Patterns and Usage in English* he lists "various concepts and how to express them." There is no attempt to be exhaustive, nor is there any criterion offered for the inclusion of those functions as opposed to any others. Hornby's chapter seems merely to reflect the awakening consciousness of the ELT profession that there is more done with words than the describing and reporting activities that tend to dominate the ELT class.

The philosophical works of Austin (1962) and Searle (1969) also concern themselves with the ways in which formal linguistic devices are employed to express meaning. This has led to the notion of the speech act (Searle, 1969) which contains both a propositional content (i.e., *what* it is that is being talked about, the locutionary force) and an illocutionary force (i.e., the communicative value the utterance has in the stream of discourse). While it is a simple matter to specify the propositions being dealt with, it is a different story when it comes to specifying the illocutionary force of an act.

Austin distinguishes among the locutionary, the illocutionary, and the perlocutionary forces of a speech act. Briefly, these performative forces correspond to *what* is being said, *how* it is intended to be taken, and *what* is brought about by it.

Searle (1975) is concerned with performative utterances and the felicity conditions under which they achieve their effects. He is also exercised by Austin's locutionary/illocutionary distinction.

Perhaps it would be possible to characterize each speech act by assigning one or more of the functions of language that Jacobson (1960) describes as relating to particular aspects of the code. According to Jacobson, (1) if the text emphasizes the addresser, its function is emotive, expressive, and affective; (2) if the text emphasizes the addressee, its function is conative, an inclination to act purposefully in giving commands and directives; (3) if the text emphasizes the context, then its function is denotive, cognitive, and referential; (4) if the text emphasizes the message then its function is poetic; (5) if the text emphasizes human contact, then its function is phatic and has to do with interaction management; (6) if the text emphasizes the code itself, then its function is metalinguistic.

It is apparent that these six functions overlap to a large degree with Halliday's three macrofunctions (1973) and to some extent coincide with Austin's distinctions among locution, illocution, and perlocution. (See Table 5.1.)

Table 5.1   Overlapping functions of language

Jacobson	Halliday	Austin
denotive (context) (3)	ideational	locution
emotive (addresser) (1) conative (addressee) (2) phatic (contact) (5)	interpersonal	perlocution
poetic (message) (4) metalinguistic (code) (6)	textual	illocution

The application of Halliday's macrofunctions to text and discourse is clearly seen in Candlin, Kirkwood, and Moore's "Developing Study Skills in English" (1975). The most detailed exposition of the macrofunctions can be found in Leech and Svartvik's *A Communicative Grammar of English* (1975).

Discourses may be further and more delicately characterized according to Jacobson's functions.

(a) If a discourse has to do with the *speaker/writer,* as when a student writes a narrative of his or her own experience, then its function may be expressive of personal values and emotional in tone. It may tend to effect a response in the reader.

(b) If a discourse has to do with the *reader,* then it most probably contains advice, commands, or directives as to how to do something.

(c) If a discourse has to do with the *message* that is part of itself, then its function is poetic. It may not relate to the world of experience in any generalized way.

(d) If a discourse has to do with keeping the *channels of communication* open, as do the personal letters we send periodically to members of our family and friends, then its function is to manage the socially-necessary interaction that our culture demands, It is phatic.

(e) If a discourse has to do with the *language* itself, then it has a metalinguistic function. It has the form that we expect in language-classroom language. Unlike baby-talk, the language we use when we talk to babies, classroom language is mostly teacher-talk. If baby-talk is the way we talk to babies, then teacher-talk ought to be the way we talk to teachers, but the term has come to mean the way teachers talk to students in the classroom when they are teaching. In language classes almost everything that is said has to do with the language that is being taught. Very little of what is said in language classes has to do in any real way with the world of knowledge and experience outside the classroom. Even in upper-level classes whose work is concentrated on specially-prepared materials, say, on reading English in science and technology, much of the teacher-talk is very complex and different from the target discourse (see McTear, 1975). And even the simple texts that students are concentrating on are often inauthentic. They remain bad examples of the types of discourse they are supposed to be illustrating, replete with specious content and unacceptable English (see Coulthard, 1977).

That is, most language-teaching materials are only *texts* and not *discourses* that have communicative functions. Students are served a soup of texts awash in teacher-talk.

(f) However, if a discourse emphasizes the larger *sociophysical* context that the student is in, a context that he or she shares because of previous knowledge and experience, then the function of the discourse is referentially cognitive and denotive. It has to do with the world of facts and ideas. Its parts are related logically and temporally. It is full of generality and can be interpreted in any unpredictable context.

It has long been held that the close reading of texts is the most effective way of producing a sensitivity to style and an appreciation of clarity and simplicity. Second-language students, however, have a major obstacle to overcome which native-language students do not face to the same degree. When we teach literature to native-readers, we assume that they recognize the context of situation of any piece of writing. Native-readers implicitly understand contextually-related norms, that is to say, *registers,* because of their prior experience with the language. For example, native-readers quickly learn to recognize parodies of writing styles, just as native TV-watchers derive most of the pleasure they get from television in perceiving the parody that is the central theme of almost all television programs. Their sensitivity to the subtleties of the medium have been developed over thousands of hours of close attention. They know what to expect. They can categorize programs consciously, and they debate the merits of "Wonder Woman," "The Six Million Dollar Man," and "The Incredible Hulk." They understand the discourse, register, theme, and style of any TV program that relates to their own experience.

Second-language students are often like children who have been deprived of television. If they have not experienced different registers fulfilling communicative uses, they can have no perception of the gross markers of rhetorical purposes, much less of the more subtle markers of style.

Style is a subvariety of a register. It is rather like an ideolect being a subvariety of a dialect. When a student has learned to expect certain features to be present in a given context, he or she can then appreciate the linguistic peculiarities of the text and its deviations from the contextually-related norm. By matching a text against what we expect in a register, we gain an appreciation of style.

Unfortunately, second-language students often do not have the knowledge of registers that will enable them to understand the purpose of a piece of writing, or text. But not all students have this disability. We believe that this condition exists in direct proportion to the distance of the students' native and acquired cultures from the culture of which the piece of writing, or text, is an expression. Western European students, for example, seem to have less trouble identifying registers in English than do students whose native cultures are further removed.

So there seems to be a continuum of types of ESL students. At one end are the literate and orate ESL students who have transferred their knowledge of discourse, register, and perhaps style in their native language to their use of English. Because of the process of selection, they are often superior to native-English students with whom they may be in competition.

At the other end of the scale are the illiterate and inorate ESL students who cannot recognize a discourse as a connected and self-contained text which has an instrumental or integrative purpose. They cannot tell when a discourse begins or ends, and cannot state precisely the purpose or field of the text. Register is a mystery to these students, and style in English as remote from their experience as participatory democracy is from a court jester's. Through close reading and explanation they can be brought to the point where they recognize that written texts have semantic and grammatical structure. We teachers might be able to demonstrate this structure if we understood it better ourselves.

The semantics of exposition is a very complex study that is in its infancy at the present time. Since it is now realized that the structure of paragraphs is conceived on the semantic level (Gutwinski, 1976), the question of how to describe the organization of complex discourses is receiving a lot of attention.

Much recent writing on discourse suggests that the relations between text and situation substance can be described structurally. Just as grammatical functions (subjects, objects, verbs, etc.) are exponents of concepts or identities, so are clauses exponents of points in exposition or of events in a narrative line.

The *theme* of a discourse is its overall main idea or main thread, the part of the text that has the greatest referential prominence, and which consequently organized the structure of the discourse (see Jones, 1977).

Pike and Pike (1977) have set up the referential (semantic) hierarchy of narrative structure as follows:

1. Performative Interaction
2. Story
3. Event
4. Identity

The four distinct levels are embedded within each other in a part-whole hierarchical organization. Each unit at every level (except the most primitive) may be analyzed into parts called immediate constituents, which are units of the same or different levels.

Performative Interaction might be called pragmatic speech acts or the illocutionary force of the narrative; that is, the use to which it is to be put, or the field of discourse.

The *Story* level consists of events with their backgrounds and settings and whatever else is necessary to report what happened.

The *Event* level consists of the relationships among the identities—the people, places, and things of the story.

The *Identities* are the primitives of the narrative.

Jones (1977), following the Pikes, sets up the referential hierarchy for expository writing.

Narrative	*Exposition*
1. Performative Interaction	1. Performative Interaction
2. Story	2. Script
3. Event	3. Point
4. Identity	4. Concept

At first glance it seems improbable that *Performative Interaction* dominates what happens in expository writing, but a moment's reflection should suffice to convince oneself that the reader is always in the writer's mind, and the reader is engaged in a kind of conversation with the writer while reading.

Expository *scripts* are analogous to and often overlapping with stories. Scripts differ from stories, we think, in that they are not always sequential. Rather they present facts and observations in a complex network of interpropositional relations which are not necessarily sequential like the events of a story. They depend on several kinds of logic, and upon the register. The presentation of comparison, contrast, description, paraphrase, evaluation, explanation, syllogism, definition, etc., depends on the field of discourse, or Performative Interaction, that dominates it.

Points are the constituents of scripts. They are analogous to events in a narrative. Points can consist of logical units such as presuppositions, arguments, and theorems. They are the main statements that show how the concepts of the exposition are related. They form the themes that make up scripts.

Concepts are shaped into points. Concepts are the lowest units of the semantic hierarchy. Concepts are clusters of meaning features. They have constituent structure. Of course, there are identities at the same level as concepts in expository discourse.

How can we recognize these constituents of the referential hierarchy? The answer is that there is normally isomorphism between the semantic and grammatical categories. The semantic constituents are usually expounded by grammatical structures.

Table 5.2 Narrative and expository referential hierarchies and their exponents in grammar

Reference (Semantics)		Grammar
Narrative	*Exposition*	
Performative	Performative ⟶	Exchange/Conversation
Story	Script ⟶	Paragraph/Section/Monologue
Event	Point ⟶	Clause/Sentence (Proposition)
Identity	Concept ⟶	Word/Phrase (Predicate, Variable, Term)

Table 5.2 (adpated from Jones, 1977) shows the similarity between the narrative and expository referential hierarchies and their exponents in grammar.

Words and phrases make up the clauses and sentences, or *grammatical constructions* of a discourse. Identities and concepts make up the events and points, or *referential configurations* of a discourse. Referential configurations are networks of events and points that constitute stories and scripts.

The purpose of this display is to show that semantics and grammar are separate and indivisible. It is of course what we mean that controls what we say. The *theme,* or main idea of a point or event consists of a concept or an identity. The theme of a script or story consists of a point or an event. The theme of an interaction consists of a script or a story. Similarly on the grammatical side, the theme of an exchange or conversation will be seen as a section or paragraph which summarizes the main point. Paragraphs or sections often have topic sentences which express their themes. Clauses contain the grammatical exponents of theme and rheme, sometimes called topic and comment, depending on whether the information is given or new. That is, a theme is called topic if it presents given (known) information.

The foregoing terms and ideas about the nature of *text* are being used in studies that are theoretical in nature. Textual analysis on the whole begins with a theoretical model, like the one presented above. Generally, theories of text are rational and model-centered. Much of the groundwork in these theories derives from the Prague School scholars (Firbas,

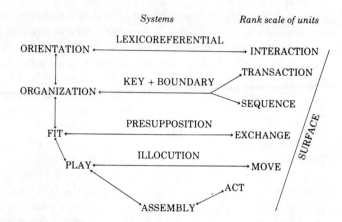

Figure 5.1 A Model for Discourse

(From *Towards an Analysis of Discourse: The English Used by Teachers and Pupils* by John McH. Sinclair and R. M. Coulthard, published by Oxford University Press 1975.)

Daneš, et al.), from Halliday and his followers, from Pike and the Summer Institute of Linguistics Tagmemicists, and from the eclectic Americans, such as the students of Lamb and Gleason.

On the other hand, what is generally known as *discourse analysis* comes from the efforts of scholars who are actually engaged in solving teaching/learning problems. These efforts are part of the descriptive tradition of the linguistics of language variation. Much of the work has a sociological basis and is concerned with the unstated rules of verbal interchange in actual conversation. It is somewhat pertinent to point out that what we are calling discourse analysis is data-centered and begins with real corpora, that is, recordings and transcriptions of language data. As such, discourse analysis is inductive in nature. It deals with empirically verifiable real-language situations. Nevertheless, theoretical models, however derived, are applied to the data in question.

In the case of Sinclair and Coulthard (1975), a rank-scale model based on Halliday's systemic grammar was applied to a classroom situation, resulting in a system of analysis that allows application to a wide range of such situations.

The reader is urged to consult the original study to see how this system works, and to consider Chapter 5, "Recent Developments," as a basic orientation to the possibilities of this sort of analysis. There its applications in education are suggested and the theories upon which it is based are discussed. In particular, the question of whether there exists well-formedness of discourse above the smallest units is broached. Additionally, "the shadowy syntactic unit *sentence*" and the results of rampant syntacticism are presented as a barrier to open-minded work on discourse. For example, if the reader can understand that "Aren't you coming?" is not the negative of "Are you coming?" he or she knows that the latter presupposes that "you" are in a position to come, but the former presupposes one or more attitudes toward your coming—disappointment, shock, sarcasm, annoyance, astonishment, and so on. Here language in its "interactive mode," that is, in its *use*, is seen as exemplary of function as opposed to form. Although evidence for formal structures higher than the sentence is plentiful, the fact that these structures are exponents of semantic categories makes the task of identifying them as such difficult. The criteria for compiling a set of features of particular functions are not clear cut—hence the search in discourse analysis for a set of *associated features* for each category of communicative function.

In a discussion of the formal exponents of the semantic systems of *phatic, indexical,* and *latent* meaning, a nice example of recognitional meaning is given:

> My information focus is a certain domestic feline quadruped that you will be able to identify positively, which at a point in time remote from the moment of this utterance had adopted a posture of lowered buttocks on a small piece of floor covering of regular dimensions, which you will also be able to identify positively. (Sinclair and Coulthard, 1975:126)

If this example were imaginary extra-terrestrial speech, or the product of a translating computer, the reader would not consider it to be unusual in its lack of words containing complexes of componential features. As it is, this sentence requires the hearer/listener to process the complex network of features in a painfully funny way, for the message seems trivial in relation to the length of the sentence. Yet much precise and technical writing is similarly exploded along componential dimensions and precisely strung together syntactically to produce discourses that often defy interpretation by readers. It is this analytical nature of much technical writing that we now turn our attention to.

When written language is componentially exploded and precisely strung together, as in the example from Sinclair and Coulthard above, and at the same time certain features of meaning are omitted or hidden, we get the kind of discourse most often found in technical writing, discourse that lacks the explicit statement of much information necessary for thorough comprehension.

The mental process by which we are able to synthesize meaning in spite of the absence of explicit information is called *inference*. Kintsch (1974) sets up three levels of difficulty of inference from stated or implied facts:

Level 1
A strong hand was needed to restrain the dog. The animal's instincts had been aroused by the sight of the fleeing deer.
(The dog is the animal)

Level 2
The burning cigarette was carelessly discarded. The fire destroyed many acres of virgin forest.
(A discarded cigarette started the fire)

Level 3
Police are hunting a man in hiding. The wife of Bob Birch disclosed illegal business practices in an interview on Saturday.
(Bob Birch is hiding)
(Bob Birch is a businessman)
(Bob Birch is guilty)
(Etc.)

(Adapted from Reder, 1978:32)

The problem that second-language learners usually encounter is that they do not totally understand a discourse even though they may understand all the words and sentences in the discourse. A part of the problem has been investigated by Lackstrom, Selinker, and Trimble, (1970) who have concerned themselves with the reading and writing problems of students in science and technology. Their efforts are concentrated on the rhetoric of English for Science and Technology (EST). What they have done is to specify the rhetorical functions of certain grammatical structures in terms of traditional rhetoric. For example, physical paragraphs do not always coincide with *sections* (or conceptual paragraphs). The problem is to help the student organize his or her understanding in spite of the discrepancies between the rhetorical form and the conceptual message.

One approach to the problem is to identify the "presuppositions" or shared (known) information necessary for comprehension, and then to teach the student to recognize implicit presuppositional information as it is called forth in the discourse, even though the information may not be given in a specific rhetorical function, such as *definition, classification, or description.*

We would suggest that teachers and course planners using the Selinker, Trimble, and Trimble scheme for the elucidation of technical (or other) discourse pay particular attention to the cover term *presupposition* as it is used here. A presupposition is information required for understanding.

Table 5.3   Rhetorical Process Chart*
             English for Science and Technology (EST)

Level	Description of Level
A	*The Objectives of the Total Discourse* EXAMPLES: 1. Detailing an experiment 2. Making a recommendation 3. Presenting new hypotheses or theories 4. Presenting other types of EST information
B	*The General Rhetorical Functions Employed to Develop the Objectives of Level A* EXAMPLES: 1. Stating purpose 2. Reporting past research 3. Stating the problem 4. Presenting information on apparatus: Description 5. Presenting information on apparatus: Operation 6. Presenting information on experimental procedures 7. Referencing an illustration 8. Relating an illustration to the discussion
C	*The Specific Rhetorical Functions Employed to Develop the General Functions of Level B* EXAMPLES: 1. Definition 2. Classification 3. Description: Physical and function 4. Description: Process
D	*The Rhetorical Techniques that Provide Relationships Within and Between the Units of Level C* EXAMPLES: 1. Time order 2. Space order 3. Causality 4. Result 5. Comparison 6. Contrast 7. Analogy 8. Exemplification

*This is a revised version of the rhetorical section of the "Rhetorical-Grammatical Process Chart" (Lackstrom, Selinker and Trimble, 1973). As this paper does not deal directly with surface grammatical forms, only the rhetorical notions are shown here. (From Selinker, Trimble, and Trimble, 1976:283. Reprinted with permission of Teachers of English to Speakers of Other Languages.)

The information may be logical or factive, as in the question "Have you stopped beating your husband?" The question presupposes that you did beat your husband, no matter whether the answer is yes or no. To presuppose something is to require an antecedent in logic or in fact. What Selinker, Trimble, and Trimble mean by *implicit presuppositional rhetorical information* is that sort of information that is buried within a rhetorical unit that is serving some explicit function other than the rhetorical unit buried within it:

> We have found in the types of discourse we have looked at that, as a rule, implicit defining information is "buried" most frequently in paragraphs whose primary rhetorical purposes are Description, Explanation, or Classification (Level C, . . .) or Presenting Information on Apparatus or on Experimental Procedures (Level B. . .). (Selinker, Trimble, and Trimble, 1976:286)

Further work on the ways information is presented in various kinds of discourse may be found in psychological studies. A good review of the work on the understanding and remembering of the content of written language is that of Reder (1978). Notably, Section 3.2, "Necessary Inferences," demonstrates the importance of general knowledge and the drawing of inferences in comprehension. Reder claims that in such studies many seminal notions are based on Grice's (1975) Co-operative Principle, in particular the necessity of finding the intended (implied) antecedent that allows comprehension of the statement under scrutiny. For example, an epithet allows the hearer/reader to bridge the gap between two statements and to determine reference:

> I met a man yesterday. The bastard wanted to stop all government support of education. (ibid., p. 61)

Obviously, to sophisticated hearer/readers, the bastard is the man, and not, say, some other person. Yet second-language students may not make this simple inference. A more complex example:

> John is a Republican. Mary is slightly daft too. (ibid., p. 62)

Are all Republicans daft? Is Mary a Republican? Would our students know the answers to these questions?

6

Toward a Theory of LSP Methodology

Martin Keith Phillips
English Language Centre
King Abdulaziz University
Jeddah, Saudi Arabia

Before undertaking a discussion of LSP methodology, I would like to raise some general considerations that will help clarify the concepts involved, and thus to formulate principles that can act as guidelines for determining what is appropriate activity in any particular LSP situation. The first and crucial notion that gives LSP its identity as a distinctive area of language teaching activity is *learner's purpose*. By learner's purpose in this context I mean an explicitly formulated behavioral objective that is not restricted to linguistic competence alone but that does involve the mastery of skills in which language forms an integral component. Typical learner's purposes in these terms are: to undertake tertiary level studies in a particular discipline through the medium of the specified language; to acquire proficiency in the formulation and execution of marketing strategy in a multi-national consumer goods-producing organization where the specified language is the medium of all or some of the relevant transactions; to be able to follow a course of training in air navigation procedures given in the specified language and to use the language in the subsequent execution of professional duties.

The purpose so defined, moreover, must be shared by all the students in the group for which an LSP course is to be designed; in other words, there must be homogeneity of purpose. Unless these two criteria, namely, the behavioral nature of the learner's purpose and its homogeneity for any particular course, are met, the situation cannot be regarded as a case of LSP, and the methodological suggestions discussed in this chapter would not apply.

In addition, the purpose must be realistic; that is, it must represent an objective attainable by the students, taking into account the constraints within which they are operating. For example, to require beginners in a language to effectively undertake university studies through the medium of that language is a realistic purpose only if sufficient resources in terms of time, manpower, and finance are allocated to the training task involved. If this condition is not fulfilled, no effective application of the methodology discussed in this chapter can be made.

In LSP, then, language is an aspect of a wider purpose; language and the learner's purpose cannot be disassociated, and to attempt to do so in an LSP course would be to try to train the student in something other than the language relating to his or her special purpose. LSP thus specifically excludes training in language skills in the abstract as a prelude to their application. In the ideal case, then, the "scope" of the LSP course would correspond to the totality of communicative events in the context defined by the student's special purpose. Since, however, such a scope is normally too broad to permit the elaboration of manageable pedagogic units, and since the student, by definition, is unable to make full and effective application of the appropriate language skills, the LSP course must set the student "enabling" objectives. These I take to be a set of lower-order behavioral objectives which, taken together, constitute the linguistic competence appropriate to the student's special purpose. I shall refer to them as "tasks." The crucial element in LSP course design is the relationship between such tasks and the behavioral objectives of the learner's purpose, as defined above.

From the foregoing it follows that any LSP task must reflect the structural characteristics of the learner's special purpose. This reflective relationship is articulated by means of the concept of "level of focus." Let us take the common case of the second-language LST situation at tertiary level. The highest level of communicative event that can meaningfully be distinguished is that of the "degree program." It would obviously be impossible to design an LST course taking this as its organizational category. At a lower level of focus, it is possible to distinguish "the course" as a communicative event. At a still lower level, one can isolate characteristic communicative units such as "set of lectures," and "series of seminars," and lower still their constituents, "the lecture," "the seminar," etc. Lower still, one distinguishes the

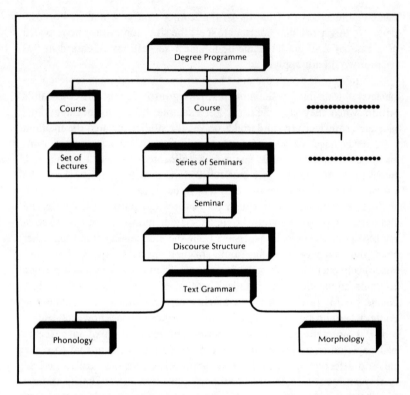

Figure 6.1   Levels of focus (communicative events) of LSP course design

discourse structure appropriate to each study mode. This leads to the analysis of the components of discourse and the text grammar of either spoken utterances or written sentences, and ultimately to the constituents of utterances at the levels of morphology and phonology. This is represented diagrammatically in Figure 6.1.

In the light of the discussion above it is now clear that in order to maintain a structural relationship between purpose and task as close as possible to the ideal case, *the upper boundary of focus of an LSP program should be at the highest level the educational system will sustain.* The lowest level of focus of that program will, then, be the lowest level of activity that derives its meaning directly from the behavioral objectives of the student's special purpose. In other words, the lower levels of activity must be generated from the upper level.

Returning to the example of university studies, the unit "course" would normally be too large to be realizable as an LSP task. It is perfectly feasible, however, to focus attention on the next level down, such as "series of seminars," or "laboratory investigation," provided these are genuine elements of the larger unit. These units are meaningful in terms of the student's special purpose, but as one analyzes further the degree of abstraction increases. With each increase in abstraction, the relationship between learner's purpose and LSP task becomes more remote, hence the task becomes less meaningful, and it becomes progressively less likely that the student will be able to operate at the higher levels of focus corresponding to his or her ultimate purpose.

It is meaningless, for example, to train air traffic control students to distinguish /æ/ and /ɑ/ either in isolation or in randomly selected words or pairs of words. It is somewhat more meaningful to train the distinction in the minimal context provided by an utterance, for example, "can take off" as opposed to "can't take off." It is, however, much more meaningful to train the student in this distinction if he or she is aware of a significant correlate of the distinction in behavioral terms; in this case, if he or she is aware that a mistake can cost lives. The distinction, therefore, has to be placed in a context where a failure to make it results in a crucial breakdown in communication. This will be discussed at greater length subsequently. The point is that lower level units become critical objects of attention only as a result of failures in communication at some higher level.

Different educational contexts have different limiting values for focus boundaries. These are determined by the variables of the particular educational situation and include at least the following: the subject content embodied in the learner's purpose; the range of the purpose in terms of skills; the duration of the LSP course; the weekly intensity of the course; the composition of the student group according to the mother tongue(s) of the students; their age; their academic background; their cultural background; their degree of competence in the L_2, if any; the staff-student ratio; the staff teaching load; the organizational structure of the educational institution; the budgetary provision for the course; and the availability of educational technology. This list is not complete and could be extended considerably by adding variables and further specifying those already listed.

With these variables in mind, there is no reason that the view outlined here should not apply to beginners. The learner variables may have consequences either for the upper level of focus that it is practicable to adopt, or alternatively for the complexity of the tasks set at the highest levels. It is not necessary, however, to adopt the position that teaching beginners is in principle a separate issue or that LSP is inappropriate in these circumstances.

While, then, individual LSP courses will differ considerably in matters of detail as a result of the particular values given to the variables of the educational situation, the notion of level of focus must be accepted in order to keep sight of the structural relationship between the learner's special purpose and the LSP course tasks. If this is lost sight of, the course is no longer an LSP course and its activities become irrelevant to the attainment of its professed objectives.

What happens when an inappropriately low level of focus is adopted can be seen by examining a widely held alternative view of language teaching procedure. This alternative can be referred to as the "analytic/synthetic approach." By this is meant a procedure by which the several skills the student must acquire are, as a matter of principle, broken down into their elementary constituents in the belief that this will enable the student, by focusing his or her attention in an ordered sequence on each element, thereby to acquire a set of abilities that can later be synthesized to form the target behavior. It is the teaching equivalent of discrete point item testing. Unless such a procedure is adopted, the argument runs, the student is faced with too integrated a situation and as a result learning is not maximally efficient, and he or she is likely to be overwhelmed by the impact of an uncontrolled body of language. Clearly this kind of argument could be used to justify LSP courses taking the lowest possible level of focus as their primary organizational principle; e.g., the level of phoneme.

There are several objections that can be raised against this point of view. First, the burden of proof of the superiority of the approach must rest with its advocates, since it proposes a more abstract relationship between purpose and task than that described here. There is no evidence to suggest that it is superior, and consequently there is no compelling reason for adopting this view. Second, there is no reason to believe that skills are analyzable into more primitive constituents; at best, complex skills could be shown to consist of aggregates of simpler skills. This of itself, however, does not justify focusing attention on the lower-order skills rather than the higher-order skill; to do so, of course, is to fail to train the higher-order skill. Moreover, the argument must rest on the concept of skills synthesis. This is usually referred to as "transfer," a notion that suggests that, in some ill-defined way, the student can, from his or her practice of isolated subskills, synthesize behavior in real communicative situations. This is most unlikely and in any case would happen only if the LSP course created the conditions under which such transfer could take place. This is, however, precisely what the adoption of too low a level of focus impedes. It is thus that the common phenomenon occurs whereby the student exhibits "language-like" behavior in the classroom but is totally inadequate in responding to the demands of a real communicative situation.

There seems to be, then, no alternative but to accept the position that I have outlined, namely, that (1) the structure of LSP tasks must be determined by the structure of the behavioral objectives of the learner's special purpose, and (2) this structure must be at the highest practicable level of focus. Acceptance of this position entails a particular methodology, by which I mean a set of principles that, when taken with contextually determined values for the variables of the particular educational situation, generate both specific teaching materials and classroom technique.

THE FIRST PRINCIPLE:
THE PRINCIPLE OF REALITY CONTROL

The view that the LSP task should be determined at the highest practicable level of focus does not mean that the student is necessarily plunged *in medias res* with no guidance from the teacher. On the contrary, it has significant implications for the manner in which tasks are rendered accessible to the student. Some of the difficulties inherent in the adoption of inappropriately low-level control measures have been seen; almost inevitably it is inimical to the reflection in the LSP task of the structure of the student's purpose. The only way in which the student's learning experience can be supportively structured without this paradox of control coming into play is to accept the principle of reality control. This principle states that:

> Control of the difficulty of the task demanded of the LSP student is exercised by means of the procedures of simplification appropriate to the field of activity constituting his or her special purpose.

It has already been argued that LSP entails the nonseparability of language, content, and operational skills. The principle of reality control states the inadmissibility of control procedures that depend on the exclusion of the parameters of the student's special purpose and, in their default, the adoption of techniques involving simplistic tinkering with the language system alone. The only forms of simplification that maintain the fidelity of the task to the student's ultimate objective are those that are normally adopted when training those skills that constitute the objective.

By way of example consider the case of a lecture note-taking course in the LST situation. Simplification can be undertaken, first, in terms of teacher input. The teacher controls variables such as pace of delivery, clarity of enunciation, and the degree to which he or she chooses to draw upon the support of visual aids. Note that all these variables appertain to the nature of the activity itself and are in no way peculiar to the LSP situation.

Second, control can be exercised by the selection of appropriate topics from the Special Purpose field. The nature of the topic determines the value of variables, such as the length of the lecture, its semantic structure (i.e., the number of the conceptual systems involved), and the nature of their relationships. In consequence the "weight" of the lexical, and to a certain extent the syntactic, load is controllable, as is the complexity of any information retrieval exercise required of the student. The essence, then, of such simplification lies in the careful selection of an appropriate topic; such selection will achieve the purpose of rendering the task accessible to the LSP student while maintaining the crucial isomorphism of the LSP task with the structure of the skill as constituent of the student's special purpose. It is thus inadmissible to attempt simplification of lexis and language structure irrespective of the systemic complexity of the special purpose objective. These points are summarized in Figure 6.2. It can now be seen how such an approach can apply equally to beginners and to students with some previous knowledge of the language. (The only condition that I would place on

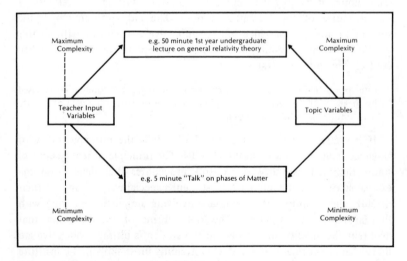

Figure 6.2 Isomorphism of LSP tasks and skills

the applicability of this approach to beginners is that they be familiar with the graphic system of the language.) The diagram in Figure 6.2 illustrates how there need be no loss in level of focus for beginners; i.e., the structure of the lecture situation is preserved, since reality control involves manipulating the parameters of the special purpose objective itself.

THE SECOND PRINCIPLE:
THE PRINCIPLE OF NONTRIVIALITY

If the learning environment is structured in the way described above, then there is no discontinuity between the LSP course tasks and the learner's special purpose objectives. In consequence the student will perceive the learning experience as meaningful activity. This is crucial to the success of any program since learning will only take place to the extent that the student feels involved in the learning process. Any control measure entails simplification, but this must not be allowed to degenerate into trivialization of the learning operations required of the student. Unfortunately this often occurs in any number of published LSP courses where the student is required to perform linguistic manipulations, apparently for their own sake, in the belief that this of itself will assist the acquisition of target skills. The following exercise, constructed but not entirely atypical, illustrates what I mean by trivilization:

Make correct sentences from the following:

The Empire State Building		twice		the British Museum
The World Trade Centre	is	three times	as high as	the Post Office Tower
The Sears Tower		four times		St. Paul's Cathedral
The Chrysler Building		etc.		my house

We have thus arrived at a second methodological principle which can be stated as follows:

> The learning tasks required of the student must be nontrivial; that is, they must be perceived by the student as meaningfully generated by his or her special purpose.

To give students of LST, for example, a task of the type, "turn the following sentences into the passive" is trivial since the *conversion* of active sentences into their passive "equivalents" is not generated by their special purpose. The *formation* of passive sentences, on the other hand, is so generated, since mastery of the formal written report form is an important requirement. As a consequence, however, this task will only be perceived by the student as meaningful if it is required of him or her as a result of a laboratory investigation that the student has undertaken. It is in this context, therefore, that it should be practiced.

This principle leads to an important distinction that should be imminent in the objectives of any unit of LSP activity—the distinction between the overt and the covert objectives of a lesson. The teacher is interested in the quality of the student's operation; the student, however, will only be motivated to perform the required operations if he or she perceives an immediate relevance to his or her concerns in the task presented. Thus the overt objective is what the student perceives; for example, the utility value of a body of information relating to the subject matter of the student's special purpose. This, however, if taken alone, would result in a course in the subject matter of a particular discipline and consequently the objectives of the LSP course would not necessarily be met. The covert objective is to maximize the student's proficiency in a skill or skills forming part of the student's special purpose. This can be done by structuring the learning experience so that the student can only acquire the information perceived as valuable by practicing those skills that constitute critical elements of his or her special purpose objective. Again, taken in isolation, the covert objective could generate practice that is trivial in the eyes of the student, as in the example above of the conversion of active into passive sentences.

As an illustration I shall take a case from the field of Languages for Occupational Purposes. Many programs for businesspeople contain a component designed to train them in the language skills involved in conducting business meetings. In one unit of one such course, the information content could relate, for example, to the relative cost-effectiveness of the manufacture of toothpicks by alternative processes. The instructions to the students to operate upon this information would take the form of a directive to the group to evaluate the two processes and to make a recommendation regarding the optimum choice. The covert objective of such a unit is clearly to oblige the students to practice skills of verbal interaction; these would involve the ability to state attitude; i.e., to agree, disagree, develop, or criticize a point of view, and the mastery of typical discussion ploys such as opening and interruption techniques. Note, however, that these would not be focused on specifically unless a breakdown in the discussion can be attributed to an inadequacy in their use. This is necessarily so since it is the overt objective (that is, the instruction to evaluate and make decisions based on the data), that the businesspeople perceive as relevant to their interests. They will, indeed, only gain practice in the language skills if they believe they are undertaking the evaluation exercise and believe in it. The second principle could be stated as a credibility rule.

THE THIRD PRINCIPLE:
THE PRINCIPLE OF AUTHENTICITY

The requirement of nontriviality limits the amount of linguistic simplification that can take place. Clearly a point is reached beyond which further simplification of the language results in trivialization of the subject matter and hence infringement of the condition of nontriviality. Consequently, in order to maintain this principle, it is necessary to accept a further principle which can be called the principle of authenticity. It can be stated as follows:

> The language that the student acquires through following the LSP course must be authentic; that is, it must be the language naturally generated by his or her special purpose.

It is not necessary to justify this principle at great length since it follows from the condition of nontriviality and from the principle of reality control; if these are accepted, then authenticity of linguistic content is entailed.

It will be illuminating, however, to pursue two related points which frequently arise in discussions of LSP. The first of these is the role of register studies, by which I mean the academic discipline that is concerned with the identification and description of areas of language use, such as the "language of physics" as opposed to the "language of football commentary." It should be clear by now that such studies are addressed to only a limited aspect of the LSP enterprise; they can certainly help to sensitize teachers and course designers to the characteristics of the authentic discourse generated by LSP courses implemented along the lines proposed in this chapter. They are, however, in no sense in themselves an adequate basis for the design of an LSP course. This point must be made because LSP course designers often confuse categories of linguistic analysis with the pedagogic principles of course design. It is thus that a "linguistic fallacy" is perpetuated. Many published courses are apparently addressed only to this relatively circumscribed aspect of the problem and fail to take into account all the behavioral requirements of the special purpose objective.

Second, unless the student has an opportunity to encounter authentic examples of language use, it is unlikely that he or she will be able to achieve *autonomy* in his or her encounters with the language, by which I mean linguistic self-confidence in the face of real-life language use, born of experience of situations made as realistic as possible. This must be a major goal of any LSP methodology, even though, in LSP, language is an aspect of some wider behavioral purpose, and the amount of time normally allocated to most LSP courses is limited.

The student can be expected to cope with authentic examples of language use to the extent that the student is involved in the subject matter. In other words, the second principle, which states that the tasks required of the student must be perceived by the student as meaningfully related to his or her special purpose, is relevant. The teacher's task, therefore, must be to generate interest and enthusiasm so that this interest, of itself, is sufficient to stimulate the student to overcome the communication difficulties arising from the authenticity of the language. It is by no means clear how the student develops strategies to cope with authentic language, nor what form such strategies take with individual students. The point is, however, that, given the opportunity, students do develop such strategies, and in so doing make significant progress toward autonomy. I assume, for the purpose of the present discussion, that the difficulties of handling authentic examples of language use are greater than those posed by language samples simplified according to purely linguistic criteria. The point is by no means obvious, but a discussion of the considerations involved is not possible within the scope of this chapter.

Moreover, it must be recognized that the difficulty supposedly inherent in authentic language does not reside wholly, nor even largely, in linguistic forms, but rather is often a function of other aspects of the learning situation, such as the complexity of the concepts involved, the nature of the instructions given to the student, or the predictability of the structure of the discourse. To pursue the last point for a moment—if, for example, a reading passage is semantically transparent (that is, if one can predict the flow of information content), then the language in which the information is couched is unlikely to present a major barrier to comprehension.

THE FOURTH PRINCIPLE:
THE PRINCIPLE OF TOLERANCE OF ERROR

A consequence of the principle of authenticity is that, even though it is possible to elaborate techniques for ensuring its practicality, it may be necessary to tolerate a higher level of certain types of error in the student's language use than is usually the case in, for example, language courses that focus primarily upon linguistic form. Whether this is a serious problem or not depends entirely on the criteria adopted for assessing the significance of error.

Errors can be of three principal types: errors of content relating to imperfect knowledge of the "real world"; errors of formal adequacy; and communicative errors. The first are matters of propositional content; the second are matters of the rules of the linguistic system; the third are matters of judgment of the effectiveness of the communication achieved, if any. The principle of tolerance of error states that:

> Errors of content and of formal adequacy are to be judged as unacceptable only to the extent that they entail errors of communicative adequacy.

Thus, for example, the student who makes the statement

(1) Water boil at 100°C

is making a formal error. In the judgment, however, of most native speakers it is unlikely that this statement would be considered as failing in communication and by the criterion stated above must be deemed acceptable.

The student, however, who makes the statement

(2) Water boils at 46°C

may be making an error of content; this will be determined by the context of utterance. In this case, with no further evidence, the error would be judged unacceptable since it is difficult to be sure as to the meaning intended; i.e., there is a breakdown in communication. With the additional knowledge, however, that the student has just performed an experiment involving the reduction of the atmospheric pressure acting on the water to 0.1 atmospheres it may well be concluded that the utterance is entirely acceptable.

The student, however, who makes the statement

(3) Water boils at 98°C at sea-level

is almost certainly making an error of propositional content. As a result it is virtually impossible to assign a meaning to the utterance; there is a breakdown in communication which entails unacceptability of the error.

To eliminate totally formal errors in the student's productive use of language, considerable effort is obviously required. Moreover, it should by now be clear that such an undertaking would be to focus at too low a level of behavior and thereby to compromise the communicative value of the learning process and, in fact, to trivialize it. In certain circumstances, however, it is quite possible to specify the total elimination of formal error as a requirement for an LSP course. This may, for example, be the case where social norms of correctness are a critical parameter of the special purpose; language training for diplomats may possibly be an example where considerations of this kind apply. In that case it would enter into the objectives of the course and the principles discussed in this chapter would hold good. The elimination of all formal errors is, however, irrelevant to most behavioral situations and therefore to the objectives of most LSP courses. It would also necessitate the expenditure of considerably more resources than are usually made available for LSP activities. The elimination of content errors, on the other hand, while seldom considered part of the brief of the LSP teacher, will in practice fall within his or her field of responsibility inasmuch as he or she is crucially concerned with the establishment of nontrivial communication.

There is obviously no algorithm for determining at what point communication breaks down on account of formal errors in the linguistic code or errors of content; that this is a matter for judgment in context was seen in the example of the student equating the boiling point of water with a temperature of 46°C. It is thus precisely the role of the teacher to judge at what point intervention is necessary. In general, however, where there is a high degree of shared experience (e.g., between two specialists in a restricted field), the limit of toleration of error is relatively high. A high degree of shared experience is often a characteristic of LSP situations.

Traditionally, however, classroom activities have been designed to minimize the possibility of error so that its occurrence in, for example, a drill technique has been taken as evidence of faulty design. This position is not tenable in the field of LSP. Rather than attempt to restrict the kind of behavior the learner may exhibit in order to minimize the possibility of error, which in this context would be self-defeating, it is more realistic to opt for a policy of progressive elimination of significant error. Such an approximative approach receives support from cognitive theories of language-learning which have highlighted the role of hypothesis formation. It is suggested that, on the basis of his or her experience of the language, the learner makes hypotheses about the structure and operations of that language which he or she tests in communication with native speakers. If this communication appears to be effective and causes no breakdowns, then to that extent the learner assumes his or her hypotheses are correct and continues to apply them. This view provides a further justification for enriching the learner's linguistic environment by exposure to authentic language. The learner should therefore not be prevented from forming hypotheses, mistaken or otherwise, and from testing them in situations requiring language use, as this is an essential element in the process of achieving acceptable norms of communicative competence.

CONCLUSION

Four principles have been enunciated and discussed in terms of which a practical LSP methodology can be elaborated. These are the principles of reality control; of nontriviality; of authenticity; and of tolerance of error. It is up to individual teachers, textbook writers, and course planners to decide in the light of their specific circumstances how these principles are to be realized in classroom technique.

These principles represent a first step toward a theory of LSP methodology; like many theories in the physical sciences, they have a wide range of application and can refer to apparently very different phenomena depending on the value given to certain variables. This only the individual course designer and teacher can undertake to do; some of these variables were listed at the start of this chapter.

Until these variables are given a value, it is not possible to detail the form specific classroom activities might take. There are no ready-made answers to questions of the type: Should translation be used?; Are drills a useful method?; Can simulation techniques help? The only possible answer is: If the combined consideration of the learner's purpose, the educational context, and the principles discussed in this chapter give rise to them, then they must be deemed acceptable; otherwise they are not.

7

Formative Evaluation in Specific Purpose Program Development

Lyle F. Bachman
University of Illinois
Urbana-Champaign

In the past decade the FL profession has witnessed a more rapid expansion in the number and types of language programs than at any other time in its history, including the post-World War II period. This is particularly true in the field of Languages for Specific Purposes (LSP), in which current staffing needs of language programs in many parts of the world far exceed the supply of qualified personnel. Furthermore, this expansion has been characterized by an unheralded diversity in methodologies and approaches, so that, whereas audio-lingualism once dominated the profession, we now find situational, notional, functional, or communicative approaches, along with LSP and its variants (Language for Science and Technology, for Academic Purposes, for Occupational Purposes, and so on) being considered the "standard" models for FL programs. This expansion of language programs has brought to the profession, perhaps for the first time on a wide scale, a realization of the need for greater accountability in program development, for less reliance on theoretical models of language and language learning, and for greater responsiveness to learner needs and to the program's performance in meeting those needs. Consequently, language program developers are becoming increasingly aware of the importance of evaluation to program development as well as the inadequacies of current evaluation practices.

In the area of LSP, one is immediately impressed by the amount of thought and research devoted to assessing learners' needs and to specifying objectives. The problem of assessing students' needs has been extensively discussed by Mackay (1978), Jones and Roe (1976), Jordan (1977), and Munby (1977, 1978), to mention a few. Specification of objectives has been even more thoroughly elaborated—focus of orientation ranges from the nature of the language content or skills to be learned, to the uses for which the language skills are intended, and includes various combinations of these points of view. A survey of the literature in the field reveals that not only have these aspects of program development been the focus of general research, but also needs assessment and the specification of objectives play important roles in the actual development of LSP programs. While this careful attention to planning and design considerations may be impressive, one cannot help but notice the virtual absence of evaluation considerations in such programs. With the exception of fleeting references to the evaluation of student proficiency or achievement or the need for monitoring the learning process, one finds virtually no descriptions or explanations of evaluation procedures and results. This is not to say that evaluation is not being carried out. Case studies do contain numerous statements such as "we found in practice that . . . ," or "we were gradually awakened to the fact that . . . ," which indicate that evaluative decisions are being made in the development of LSP programs. The overall impression, however, is that such evaluation is conducted in an informal ad hoc manner, and that seldom is evaluation incorporated into the program design. Furthermore, it is my impression that this is not because LSP program developers do not see the need for such evaluation. On the contrary, discussions with colleagues in the field reveal a general feeling of dissatisfaction with current evaluation practices. It is the purpose of this chapter to discuss some of the principles and considerations in program evaluation, to describe a number of evaluation procedures that have proven useful, and, above all, to dispel some of the mystique and distrust that often surround evaluation.

PURPOSE OF EVALUATION: DECISION-MAKING

When discussing the role of evaluation in LSP programs it is useful to bear in mind a number of considerations regarding evaluation in general. Evaluation, essentially, is the collection and use of information for the purpose of decision-making. It is this purpose that characterizes evaluation and distinguishes it from testing and measurement. Although tests and other forms of measurement are commonly among the methods used for gathering information, they are not, in themselves, evaluative. Data derived through such procedures become evaluative only when they are used as input to the decision-making process. It is essential, therefore, that evaluation be conducted within a specific framework of decision alternatives.

LEVELS OF EVALUATION

In any educational program there are innumerable decisions, at various levels, to be made, and each decision involves the consideration of numerous alternatives. The roles of evaluation in educational programs can be best understood, I believe, by considering the level of the decisions contingent upon the evaluation. At one level there are decisions to be made regarding individuals in the program. Students are evaluated in order to determine their readiness for specific programs, the rate at which they should proceed through these programs, and the acceptability of their achievement to teachers, administrators, peers, prospective employers, and to society in general. Teachers and administrators are likewise evaluated with regard to their suitability for and performance of specific duties and responsibilities. At another level are decisions regarding the program itself—its effectiveness, efficiency, acceptability, even its reason for existing. Information relevant to both these levels of evaluative decisions could be provided, for example, by the results of a reading achievement test administered at the completion of part of a given program. As a diagnosis of student achievement in reading, individual scores might be used to make decisions regarding advancement or retention of individual students in the program, or their placement into a remedial component. Group averages on the test and its parts might, on the other hand, indicate weaknesses in specific components of the program or in the program as a whole, and therefore provide information for making decisions about revising the program itself. This distinction between micro-evaluation, or the evaluation of individuals, on the one hand and macro-evaluation, or the evaluation of programs, on the other, does not imply, however, that the two are independent. Decisions regarding individuals are invariably contingent upon program considerations. Witness, for example, the wide range of admission, grading, and employment practices among American colleges and universities alone, not to mention institutions in other countries. Similarly, no program evaluation can afford to ignore the evaluation of the individuals in that program.

TYPES OF EVALUATION

Another distinction is that which has been made between formative and summative evaluation (Scriven, 1967). At the program level, *formative evaluation* provides information and feedback during the development of the program in order to facilitate decision-making regarding the improvement of content, organization, strategies, and techniques. *Summative evaluation,* on the other hand, more typically deals with "completed" programs and is directed toward decisions concerning, for example, the wider implementation of a given program, the continuation or discontinuation of a program, or the adoption of one of several competing programs. Both formative and summative evaluation play an important role in making decisions about educational programs, but it is my belief that one of the most pressing current needs in the area of LSP is for more systematic formative evaluation in developing programs.

FORMATIVE EVALUATION

As indicated above, the primary purpose of formative evaluation is to provide information for making judgments regarding the revision and improvement of instructional programs while they are in the process of development. Formative evaluation is concerned, therefore, not only with the results of the program, but, more directly, with how the program produces its effects and what conditions limit or facilitate its effectiveness. Although formative evaluation is thus inseparable from the process of program development, not every developing program is suitable for formative evaluation. The first consideration to be made in planning formative evaluation, therefore, is the suitability of the program for such evaluation. A program must be both describable and repeatable if the interpretation of data and recommendations for revision are to be applicable. A program is describable if its goals and objectives are precisely stated in operational terms and if it incorporates processes that can be clearly defined. A program is repeatable only if it does not rely heavily on the specific abilities of a particular teacher or on a unique set of conditions that cannot be replicated elsewhere. Programs not meeting these requirements will obviously be difficult to evaluate adequately, because of the poor likelihood of obtaining data that will be of use in improving the program. Such programs are unsuitable for the kind of formative evaluation discussed below.

A second consideration is that of the evaluation design. In order to be effective, the evaluation design should enable the program developer to obtain pertinent information on both the effects and instructional processes, and to relate these two types of data to each other so that appropriate changes in the program can be made. That is, if the evaluation is well-designed, the program developer should be able to determine what causal relationships, if any, exist between the learning and teaching activities that comprise the program and the observed outcomes of the program.

A third consideration is the specific kinds of data that need to be gathered. This will depend, of course, on the decisions to be made. Data on irrelevant areas or areas we cannot do anything about may be interesting, but of little use for formative evaluation. Standardized tests, for example, which typically yield normed scores, seldom provide information pertinent to program improvement. This is because such tests are designed and developed to measure a broad range of skills, and seldom do their objectives match the specialized objectives that typify LSP programs.

A final consideration concerns sample size. Here the best rule of thumb is to start with a small group—a single class or less—and expand as the program develops. The time and effort required to process large bodies of data often impede the development of the program itself. Furthermore, decisions regarding revisions in developing programs are typically based on a careful scrutiny of both test and observational data, and seldom on statistical significance, so large samples are usually not essential for purposes of formative evaluation.

The process of formative evaluation parallels that of program development, and comprises two types of activity: the internal assessment of what the program is supposed to be, and the gathering and interpretation of external information during field-testing. The requisites for both these activities are needs assessment and the specification of objectives.[1] Given a particular objective set, one aspect of internal assessment is to evaluate these objectives themselves. Is the rationale for each objective cogent? Are there undesired consequences associated with achieving certain objectives? Are any of the objectives in conflict with higher educational or social values? Are the objectives generally acceptable to relevant groups and to specialists? Another aspect of internal assessment is a content-based review. Are the materials accurate? Do they comprise an appropriate range, in both difficulty and interest, vis-à-vis the learner? Or are any of the expected outcomes not accounted for in the instructional process?

Once the developer is satisfied, on the basis of the internal assessment, that the program incorporates the intended objectives and processes, he or she must then determine how it can most effectively produce the intended outcomes. This typically involves field-testing. Note that evaluation-based program development is normally cyclical, proceeding from the small-scale try-out of an instructional prototype, or representative component of the program, to the operational testing of the entire program. At the prototype stage, when the primary concern is with successfully achieving the set objectives, and the developer is frequently the teacher, the primary sources of data are students' performance, students' reactions, and observers' reactions. Techniques for measuring student performance outcomes have been extensively discussed in the literature on testing; they include multiple-choice, completion, cloze, and dictation tests, not to mention oral interviews. These procedures are well-known, and require no further elaboration here. Data on the processes students employ in learning can be obtained through the use of practice exercises, worksheets, programmed learning sequences, and systematic observation. Data on student reactions to the program can be gathered via questionnaires, scaling procedures, interviews, and observations. Specialists' and other observers' reactions to the program, with regard to both effects and processes, provide a valuable source of evaluation data, particularly at the prototype stage, when the developer as teacher may fail to notice important deficiencies through lack of objectivity.

In operational field-testing or trialling, the primary concern of formative evaluation is to determine the effectiveness of the program under relatively natural conditions (Baker, 1974). Here the concerns of setting and sample size become more critical. For the results of operational trialling to be generalizable, the setting must approximate as closely as possible that for which the program is intended. Since teacher and administrative variables become important at this stage, the sample size will need to be larger and to comprise more classes and, in some cases, more than one administrative unit. A large sample size at this stage makes procedures such as matrix sampling feasible, thus facilitating the evaluation of program effects. In addition to the data sources available at the prototype stage, other sources—teachers' performance, and the reactions of teachers, administrators, and the speech community—become important in operational trialling. Data on the processes teachers employ are useful for determining the degree to which teachers adhere to the strategies and procedures of the program, to identify better teaching practices, and to determine needs for teacher training. This sort of data can often be best obtained through direct observation, using a checklist of critical points (Flanders, 1970; Ross-Sheriff, 1975). The reactions of students, teachers, administrators, and the speech community to the program can be effectively obtained through questionnaires, rating scales, interviews, and periodic meetings among these parties and the developers.

DOMAIN-REFERENCED TESTS

Throughout this discussion, various data collection procedures have been mentioned, in the context of the types of data useful for formative evaluation. It seems appropriate at this point to elaborate on two procedures that may serve as correctives to current practices and that may improve our capability for gathering student-reaction data. In the majority of LSP programs some sort of objective testing procedures are used, the most common being criterion-referenced achievement tests, usually administered to groups of students at the end of the program, as well as at various periods throughout the program, and sometimes as pre-tests. In addition to these achievement tests, program developers frequently employ standardized norm-referenced tests. Many evaluators feel, however, that neither of these testing procedures is adequate for the purposes of formative evaluation (Cronbach, 1967; Millman, 1974). Standardized tests may provide interesting information regarding individual students in the program, but they seldom measure the specific content or skills included in the program, and therefore provide little, if any, information relevant to program revision. Criterion-referenced tests, as they are normally given, with all students taking the same test or at best two parallel forms of the same test, generally provide valid information only about individual student achievement in the program. The relatively small amount of content that can be tested this way limits the information available for formative evaluation. The technique of domain-referenced testing, on the other hand, enables the evaluator to sample the content and skills areas of the program much more extensively (Millman, 1974). Suppose, for example, that one "domain" in an LSP program is defined as follows: "understanding relations between parts of a text through lexical cohesion devices," and that this domain comprises the following subskills: "repetition, synonymy, hyponymy, antithesis, apposition, lexical set/collocation, and pro-forms/ general words" (Munby, 1978). With, say, ten classes of twenty students each, the criterion-referenced procedure for testing mastery of these sub-objectives might be to develop a test of, perhaps, fifteen items, with approximately two items for each sub-objective. Interpreting the results of this test, the program developer could determine, with reasonable assurance, which students had or had not mastered these objectives. But suppose that the results are generally poor: 80 percent of the students score below 70 percent. Assuming that the test itself is valid and reliable, what information can be derived from the test results to enable the program developer to improve the program? To pinpoint areas of weaknesses, item analysis is appropriate. But given the testing procedure, even with a relatively large number of student responses (200 x 15 = 3,000), only a small sampling (15) of performance on the objectives is available. One solution to this problem would be to write a longer test, with more items per objective. But there is an obvious limit to this procedure, in terms of the ratio of testing to teaching time. Another solution would be to prepare a population or "bank" of test items covering the domain and to prepare multiple forms of the test, each form containing a different set of items, selected from the item population by random or stratified random sampling. The increase in the sampling of student performance data on the objectives can easily be seen in the above example, where, by preparing two forms of the test and giving each form to half the students, the sampling of the objectives is doubled, without increasing either the size of the student sample or the length of the test. This principle underlies the method of matrix sampling, whereby different groups of students are systematically given different sets of test items, so as to insure representative sampling of both students and items, and to maximize the amount of program content tested within a given sample size (Sirotnik, 1974). The major advantage of domain-referenced testing, then, is that it allows the evaluator to collect the maximum amount of student performance data on the objectives of the program (as well as data on effects not included in the objectives), and at the same time, to estimate individual student domain scores or "true levels of functioning." Data from domain-referenced tests are thus relevant to both program and individual evaluation. Furthermore, the precision with which objectives and sub-objectives can be specified in LSP programs provides an ideal basis for the development and use of this testing procedure.

RATING SCALES

To obtain information regarding teacher and student reactions to programs, questionnaires are commonly used. It has been my experience, however, that neither teachers nor students can be expected to answer questionnaires with either the perspective or the specificity required by the evaluator. While specific comments on the merits or failings of a given component frequently provide invaluable information for revising the program, the amount of useless verbiage that must be sifted through to obtain these few nuggets of information usually vitiates the usefulness of even the best-designed questionnaire. A much more effective procedure, I believe, is the use of rating scales which focus on specific components and qualities of the program. The use of such a rating scale has been reported by Bachman, Amirhor, and Weidhmann (1977). Using this scale, a portion of which is presented in Table 7.1, teachers and

Table 7.1   Sample rating form

	Use	Int.	Length	Diff.
Reading passage A	1 2 3 4	1 2 3 4	1 2 3 4	1 2 3 4
Reading passage B	1 2 3 4	1 2 3 4	1 2 3 4	1 2 3 4
Comp. exercise	1 2 3 4	1 2 3 4	1 2 3 4	1 2 3 4
Vocab. exercise	1 2 3 4	1 2 3 4	1 2 3 4	1 2 3 4
Instructs/explanats	1 2 3 4	1 2 3 4	1 2 3 4	1 2 3 4

students are asked to rate program components such as reading passages, comprehension exercises, vocabulary exercises, and instructions/ explanations according to specific qualities (usefulness, interest, length, and difficulty) that the developers consider important to the effectiveness of the program. Ratings, made by circling the appropriate number for each component and quality, are as follows: 1 = bad, 2 = unacceptable, 3 = acceptable, and 4 = good. Teachers are asked to complete the ratings for materials covered after each class period, while students are asked to rate components after each unit of instruction. Respondents are also asked to write comments, particularly on those components they have rated as either bad or unacceptable. The advantages of such rating forms are their comprehensiveness, convenience, and efficiency for collecting specific data concerning the effectiveness of the program, as well as ease of analysis. Arithmetic means can be computed for each component across all qualities, for each quality across all components, and for the entire lesson. These average ratings can then be used to pinpoint areas where revision is necessary. Respondents' comments, along with interviews and round-table discussions among teachers and developers, are then used to determine how these problem components can best be revised.

Data collection procedures, particularly testing and scaling, are often surrounded with an aura of complexity, and evaluation is frequently associated with elaborate research designs; but it should be emphasized that, for purposes of program development or materials preparation, this need not be the case. As indicated above, the amount and type of information gathered should be determined by the kinds of decisions to be made. In the majority of programs perhaps the most useful information is of an informal and subjective nature. This is not to say, however, that it cannot be systematic. Whatever the nature of the information collected for evaluation, it must meet the requisites that it cover the content of the program and enable the developer to relate outcomes to processes. Regarding the procedures for collecting and analyzing formative evaluation data, carefully controlled experimental or quasi-experimental designs are seldom warranted; nor are elaborate statistical procedures such as analysis of variance and covariance or regression analysis. This is because the decisions to be made seldom impinge on the results produced by these procedures. If we are interested, for example, in revising a reading passage considered useful and interesting, but too difficult for students at a given level, of what use is it to know that students using our materials scored significantly better on a given reading test than students in a "control" group who are using different materials, and perhaps a different approach to reading?

RESPONSIBILITY FOR EVALUATION

The above discussion has dealt primarily with *what, how,* and, to some extent, *when* to evaluate. But equally important is the question of *who* does the evaluation. It has been argued on the one hand that, in order to avoid biases and to maintain objectivity, evaluation should not be carried out by the program developers themselves. Furthermore, it is claimed, the program development staff normally lacks the expertise to carry out valid evaluation. On the other hand, program developers frequently complain that independent evaluators, both in-house and external, do not understand the program objectives or instructional strategies will enough to be able to evaluate them, and often evaluate programs against criteria that are not relevant. All of these arguments are valid, and unfortunately the current orientation in LSP, and in SL/FL in general, toward evaluation as testing and grading, and the frequent use of standardized tests, which often yield results that are either of no use or at best equivocal, have made it difficult to convince program developers that formative evaluation is not only important, but also "doable." The answer to this problem of who carries out the evaluation function lies in Cronbach's assertion that "formative evaluation is a fundamental part of curriculum development, not an appendage" (1967:18). For a number of reasons, the program development staff itself is in the best position to carry out formative evaluation. First, from a very practical point of view, they are normally available, so that the turn-around time for the utilization of evaluation data is generally much shorter than if the evaluation were done externally. Second, the development staff is more likely to know what the decision alternatives for revision are; that is, what instructional options are available in the program. Finally, the developers themselves are in a better position to know what kind of evaluation information they really need, and how best to make use of it. Objectivity is less of a problem in formative than in summative evaluation, but the lack of evaluation expertise among program developers and the problem of specifying appropriate evaluation criteria are genuine concerns. While current research in LSP needs assessment is rapidly developing objective frameworks suitable for systematic evaluation, only through the inclusion of such evaluation in developing programs will program developers acquire sufficient experience for evaluation to be regarded without suspicion as essential to program development.

NOTE

1. Needs assessment and the specification of objectives are normally conducted as the first steps in the evaluation process. These steps, particularly in the latter, are described in detail by Bachman and Strick (Chapter 3).

REFERENCES

Abercrombie, D. "Linguistics and the teacher," in *Problems and Principles in Language Study.* London: Longman, 1956.

Aiken, P. L., and L. F. Bachman. *Individualizing EFL: Curriculum Research and Development in Thailand.* Bangkok: Central Institute of English Language, 1977.

Allen, J. P. B., and H. G. Widdowson. "Teaching the communicative use of English," in R. Mackay and A. Mountford (eds.), *English for Specific Purposes.* London: Longman, 1978.

Austin, J. L. *How to Do Things with Words.* Oxford, England: Clarendon, 1962.

Bachman, L. F., J. Q. Amirhor, and W. E. Weidhmann. "Reading English discourse: Materials for business administration, economics, law and political science." Paper presented at the Second Regional Conference on ESP, Isfahan, Iran, 1977.

Bachman, L. F., and G. J. Strick. "A theoretical model for ESP program design." Paper presented at the Twelfth Annul TESOL Convention, Mexico City, 1978.

Bachman, L. F., and G. J. Strick. "An analytical approach to language program design." Paper presented at the Twelfth Annual TESOL Convention, Mexico City, 1978.

Baker, E. "Formative evaluation of instruction," in W. J. Popham (ed.), *Evaluation in Education: Current Applications.* Berkeley: McCutchan, 1974.

Barzun, J., and H. F. Graff. *The Modern Researcher.* New York: Harcourt Brace, 1957.

Bates, M. "Writing 'Nucleus'," in R. Mackay and A. Mountford (eds.), *English For Specific Purposes.* London: Longman, 1978.

Bates, M., and T. Dudley-Evans. "General science," in *Nucleus,* including Agriculture, Biology, Chemistry, Engineering, etc. London: Longman, 1976.

Bloom, B. J., J. T. Hastings, and G. F. Madaus. *Handbook on Formative and Summative Evaluation for Student Learning.* New York: McGraw-Hill, 1971.

Bojar, R. B. "Foreign Service Institute's first summer intern program," in *Linguistic Reporter,* Vol. 7, No. 6 (December, 1965), pp. 1-2.

Brooks, C., and R. K. Warren. *Modern Rhetoric* (3rd Edition). New York: Harcourt Brace & World, 1970.

Candlin, C. N., J. M. Kirkwood, and H. M. Moore. "Developing study skills in English," in EAS, *ETIC Occasional Paper.* London: The British Council, 1975.

Candlin, C. N., J. M. Kirkwood, and H. M. Moore. "Study skills in English: Theoretical issues and practical problems," in R. Mackay and A. Mountford (eds.), *English for Specific Purposes.* London: Longman, 1978.

Candlin, C. N., J. H. Leather, and C. Bruton. "Doctors in casualty: Applying communicative competence to components of specialist course design," in *IRAL,* Vol. 14., No. 3 (August, 1976).

Cao-Romero, L. *Functiones en la Organizacion de Informacion de Textos Tecnicocientificos* (Mimeographed). Fac. de Filosofia y Letras, UNAM, Mexico City, 1976.

Casson, M. *Introduction to Mathematical Economics.* London: Nelson, 1973.

Catford, J. C. *A Linguistic Theory of Translation,* London, Oxford U. Press, 1965.

Chatman, S. "New ways of analyzing narrative structure," in *Language and Style,* 1968-69.

Chiu, R. K. "Measuring register characteristics: A prerequisite for preparing advanced level TESOL programs," in *TESOL Quarterly,* Vol. 6, No. 2, 1975.

Corder, S. P. *Introducing Applied Linguistics.* London: Penguin Education, 1973.

Coulthard, M. "Discourse analysis in English—A short review of the literature," in *Language Teaching and Linguistics: Abstracts,* Vol. 8, No. 2, Cambridge University Press (April, 1975).

Coulthard, M. *An Introduction to Discourse Analysis.* London: Longman, 1977.

Cowie, A. P., and J. B. Heaton. *Preparing a Writing Programme for Students of Science and Technology.* (Mimeographed) University of Leeds, 1975.

Criper, C. "Linguistics, sociolinguistics and current trends in communication-based syllabuses," in G. H. Wilson (ed.), *Curriculum Development and Syllabus Design for English Teaching.* Singapore: Regional English Language Center, 1976.

Cronbach, L. J. "Evaluation for course improvement," in *Teachers College Record,* 64, pp. 672-683, 1963.

Cronbach, L. J. "Course improvement through evaluation," in R. E. Stake (ed.), *Perspectives on Curriculum Evaluation* (AERA Monograph Series on Curriculum Evaluation, No. 1). Chicago: Rand McNally, 1967.

Crymes, R. H. "The developing art of TESOL: Theory and practice," in C. H. Blatchford and J. Schachter (eds.), *On TESOL '78: EFL Policies, Programs, Practices.* Washington, D.C.: TESOL, 1978.

Crystal, D., and D. Davy. *Investigating English Style.* London: Longman, 1969.

Dakin, J. *Language Laboratory and Language Learning.* London: Longman, 1973.

Davies, A. "Do foreign students have problems?" in A. P. Cowie and J. B. Heaton (eds.), *English for Academic Purposes,* pp. 34-36. Reading: British Association for Applied Linguistics, 1977.

Derwing, B. L., N. W. Schutz, and C. M. Yang. *Project on English for Students of Science and Technology in the Republic of China.* Corvallis: Oregon State University, ESP Clearinghouse, 1977.

Ellis, M., and T. Kirk. *AIT Reading and Writing Program* (Mimeographed). Bangkok: Asian Institute of Technology, 1976.

Enkvist, N. E. "On defining style," in J. Spencer (ed.), *Linguistics and Style.* London: Oxford University Press, 1964.

Firth, J. R. *Papers in Linguistics, 1934-51.* London: Oxford University Press, 1957.

Flanders, N. A. *Analyzing Teaching Behaviors.* Reading, Mass.: Addison-Wesley, 1970.

Gleason, H. A., Jr. "Contrastive analysis in discourse structure," in *Monograph Series on Languages and Linguistics,* No. 21, pp. 39-63, 1968.

Gregory, M. "Aspects of varieties differentiation," in *Journal of Linguistics,* Vol. 3, No. 2, 1967.

Grice, H. P. "Logic and conversation," in P. Cole and J. Morgan (eds.), *Syntax and Semantics (Vol. 3): Speech Acts.* New York: Academic Press, 1975.

Gumperz, J. J. "The speech community," in *International Encyclopedia of the Social Sciences,* pp. 381-386. New York: Macmillan, 1968.

Gumperz, J. J., and D. Hymes (eds.), *Directions in Sociolinguistics.* New York: Holt, Rinehart and Winston, 1972.

Gutwinski, W. *Cohesion in Literary Texts, A Study of Some Grammatical and Lexical Features of English Discourse.* The Hague: Mouton, 1976.

Halliday, M. A. K. *Explorations in the Functions of Language.* London: Edward Arnold, 1973.

Halliday, M. A. K., and R. Hasan. *Cohesion in English*. London: Longman, 1976.
Halliday, M. A. K., A. McIntosh, and P. Strevens. *The Linguistic Sciences and Language Teaching*. London: Longman, 1964.
Haugen, E. "The ecology of language," in A. S. Dill (ed.), *The Ecology of Language: Essays by Einar Haugen*, pp. 325-339. Stanford: Stanford University Press, 1972.
Hawaii, State of. *Hawaii English Program: Project Evaluation Report 1971-72*. Honolulu: State Department of Education, 1972.
Hayes, A. S., W. E. Lambert, and G. R. Tucker. "Evaluation of foreign language teaching," in *Foreign Language Annals*, Vol. 1, No. 1, pp. 22-44, 1967.
Hendricks, W. O. "Current trends in discourse analysis," in *Essays on Semiolinguistics and Verbal Art*, No. 2. The Hague: Mouton, 1973.
Hendricks, W. O. *Grammars of Style and Styles of Grammar*. Amsterdam: North Holland, 1976.
Horn, V. "Advanced reading: Teaching logical relationships," in *English Teaching Forum*, Washington, D. C.: USIA, 1971.
Hornby, A. S. *A Guide to Patterns and Usage in English*. London: Oxford University Press, 1954.
Hymes, D. H. "Models of the interaction of language and social life," in J. J. Gumperz and D. Hymes (eds.), *Directions in Sociolinguistics*. New York: Holt, Rinehart and Winston, 1972.
Jacobson, R. "Closing statement: Linguistic and poetics," in T. Sebeok (ed.), *Style in Language*. Cambridge: The Technology Press of MIT, pp. 350-377. 1960.
Johns, T. F., and C. M. Johns. "The current programme of materials development in English for academic purposes at the Universities of Birmingham and Aston," in J. C. Richards (ed.), *Teaching English for Science and Technology*. Singapore: Regional English Language Center, 1976.
Jones, L. K. *Theme in English Expository Discourse*. Lake Bluff, Illinois: Jupiter Press, 1977.
Jones, K., and A. Mountford. "Some dimensions in the design of service English programmes." Paper presented at the Second Regional Conference on ESP, Isfahan, Iran, 1977.
Jones, K., and P. Roe. "Designing English for science and technology (EST) programmes," in *EAS, ETIC Occasional Paper*. London: The British Council, 1975.
Jones, K., and P. Roe. "Problems in designing programmes in English for science and technology overseas," in J. C. Richards (ed.), *Teaching English for Science and Technology*. Singapore: Regional English Language Center, 1976.
Jordan, R. R. "Identification of problems and needs: A student profile," in A. P. Cowie and J. B. Heaton (eds.), *English for Academic Purposes*. Reading: British Association for Applied Linguistics, 1977.
Jordan, R. R. "Language practice materials for economists," in R. Mackay and A. Mountford (eds.), *English for Specific Purposes*. London: Longman, 1978.
Kintsch, W. *The Representation of Meaning in Memory*. Hillsdale, N.J.: Erlbaum, 1974.
Koen, R., A. Becker, and R. Young. *The Psychological Reality of the Paragraph* (Mimeographed). Ann Arbor: University of Michigan, 1981.
Lackstrom, J. E., L. Selinker and L. Trimble. "Grammar and Technical English," in R. C. Lugton, ed., *English as a Second Language: Current Issues,* Center for Cur-

riculum Development, Inc. New York: Rand McNally, 1970. Also reprinted in *The Art of TESOL*, English Teaching Forum, Washington, D. C., 1975.

Lackstrom, J. E., L. Selinker, and L. Trimble. "Technical Rhetorical Principles and Grammatical Choice," TESOL *Quarterly*, 7, 2, 1973.

Laing, R. *The politics of Experience and the Bird of Paradise*. London; Penguin, 1973.

Lambert, W. E., and G. R. Tucker. *Bilingual Education of Children: The St. Lambert Experiment*. Rowley, Mass.: Newbury House, 1972.

Landesman, C. *Discourse and Its Presuppositions*. New Haven and London: Yale University Press, 1972.

Leech, G., and J. Svartvik. *A Communicative Grammar of English*. London: Longman, 1975.

Levin, L. *Implicit and Explicit: A Synopsis of Three Parallel Experiments in Applied Psycholinguistics, Assessing Different Methods of Teaching Grammatical Structures in English as a Foreign Language*. Gothenburg, Sweden: Gothenburg School of Education, 1971.

Lindblad, T., and L. Levin. *Teaching Grammar: An Experiment in Applied Psycholinguistics, Assessing Three Different Methods of Teaching Grammatical Structures in English as a Foreign Language*. Gothenburg, Sweden: Gothenburg School of Education, 1970.

Lindvall, C. M. "The task of evaluation in curriculum development projects: A rationale and case study," in R. E. Stake (ed.), *Perspectives on Curriculum Evaluation* (AERA Monograph Series on Curriculum Evaluation, No. 1). Chicago: Rand McNally, 1967.

Mackay, R. "Final report of the English section," in M. de Greve, M. Gorosch, C. G. Sandulescu, and F. van Passel (eds.), *Modern Language Teaching to Adults: Language for Special Purposes*. Paris: AIMAV/DIDIER, pp. 279-286, 1973.

Mackay, R. "Identifying the nature of the learner's needs," in R. Mackay and A. Mountford (eds.), *English for Specific Purposes*. London: Longman, 1978.

Mackay, R., and A. Mountford. "Reading for information," in E. M. Anthony and J. C. Richards (eds.), *Reading Insights and Approaches*. Singapore: SEAMEO RELC and Singapore University Press, 1976.

Mackay, R., and A. Mountford (eds.). *English for Specific Purposes: A Case Study Approach*. London: Longman, 1978.

Marder, D. *The Craft of Technical Writing*. New York: Macmillan, 1960.

McCrimmon, J. M. *Writing with a Purpose*. Boston: Houghton Mifflin, 1976.

McTear, M. "Potential sources of confusion in the foreign language lesson." Paper presented at Fourth AILA Congress, Stuttgart, 1975.

Millman, J. "Criterion-referenced measurement," in W. J. Popham (ed.), *Evaluation in Education: Current Applications*. Berkeley: McCutchan, 1974.

Mohan, B. "Discourse, context and language for specialized purposes," in *AILA Proceedings*, 1975.

Mohan, B. "Towards a situational curriculum," in *On TESOL '77*. Washington, D.C.: TESOL, 1977.

Moore, W. J., and L. D. Kennedy. "Evaluation of learning in the language arts," in B. S. Bloom et al. (eds.), *Handbook on Formative and Summative Evaluation of Student Learning*. New York: McGraw-Hill, 1971.

Morrison, J. "An investigation of problems in listening-comprehension encountered by overseas students in the first year of postgraduate studies in sciences in the

University of Newcastle-upon-Tyne, and the implications for teaching. M.Ed. dissertation, University of Newcastle-Tyne, England, 1974.

Munby, J. "Processing profiles of communicative needs," in *ESP: An International Symposium.* Bogota: The British Council, 1977.

Munby, J. *Communicative Syllabus Design.* London: Cambridge University Press, 1978.

Palmer, J. D. "The behaviorist in the woodpile," in *Pasaa,* a Festschrift for Richard Noss, Vol. VI, Nos. 1 and 2, Bangkok: Central Institute of English Language (October, 1976).

Palmer, J. D. "The concept of register and English for special purposes," in *SPEAQ Journal,* Vol. 1, No. 3, 1977.

Palmer, J. D., and R. Mackay. "The dimensions of English for special purposes." Unpublished paper prepared for TESOL ALSIG 1978. Montreal: TESL Centre, Concordia University, 1978.

Perren, G. E. "Introductory: The past five years," in G. E. Perren (ed.), *CILT Reports and Papers,* pp. 7-11. London: Centre for Information on Language Teaching, 1974.

Phillips, B. "Structure in discourse," in *The Second LACUS Forum, 1975,* pp. 381-399. Columbia, S.C.: The Hornbeam Press, 1976.

Phillips, M. K., and C. C. Shettlesworth. "How to arm your students: A consideration of two approaches to providing materials for ESP," in *English for Specific Purposes.* ELT Documents. London: The British Council, 1978.

Pike, K. L. "Discourse analysis and tagmemic matrices," in *Oceanic Linguistics,* Vol. 3, pp. 5-25, 1964.

Pike, K. L., and E. G. Pike. *Grammatical Analysis.* Summer Institute of Linguistics, Normon, Oklahoma, 1977.

Portwood, C. S. "An analytic approach to the selection of a curriculum development design." Paper presented at the Third Annual Conference on Educational Research, Bangkok, Thailand, 1976a.

Portwood, C. S. "The ideal model of curriculum development." Paper presented at the Third Annual Conference on Educational Research, Bangkok, Thailand, 1976b.

Reder, L. M. *Comprehension and Retention of Prose: A Literature Review.* Cambridge, Mass.: Bolt, Beranek and Newman, 1978.

Ross-Sheriff, F. "Direct observations of behaviors and interactions in individualized classrooms," in L. F. Bachman (ed.), *Individualized Instruction (Pasaa,* Special Issue, Vol. 5, No. 1). Bangkok: Central Institute of English Language, 1975.

Sacks, H. *Typescript of Classroom Lectures* (Mimeographed). Irvine: University of California, 1967.

Sacks, H. "On the analyzability of stories by children," in J. J. Gumperz and D. Hymes (eds.), *Directions in Sociolinguistics.* New York: Holt, Rinehart and Winston, 1972.

Sanders, J. R., and D. J. Cunningham. "A structure of formative evaluation in product development," in *Review of Educational Research,* Vol. 43, No. 2, pp. 217-236, 1973.

Sapir, E. *Language.* New York: Harcourt Brace, 1921.

Schegloff, E. A. "Sequencing in conversational openings," in *American Anthropologist,* Vol. 10, No. 6, pp. 1075-1095, 1968.

Scriven, M. "The methodology of evaluation," in R. E. Stake (ed.), *Perspectives on*

Curriculum Evaluation (AERA Monograph Series on Curriculum Evaluation, No. 1). Chicago: Rand McNally, 1967.

Scriven, M. "Evaluation perspectives and procedures," in W. J. Popham (ed.), *Evaluation in Education: Current Applications.* Berkeley: McCutchan, 1974.

Searle, J. R. *Speech Acts.* London: Cambridge University Press, 1969.

Searle, J. R. "Indirect speech acts," in P. Cole and J. Morgan (eds.), *Syntax and Semantics (Vol. 3): Speech Acts.* New York: Academic Press, 1975.

Selinker, L., and L. Trimble. *Technical Communication for Foreign Engineering Students* (Mimeographed). Seattle: University of Washington College of Engineering, 1968.

Selinker, L., R. M. T. Trimble, and L. Trimble. "Presuppositional rhetorical information in ESL discourse," in *TESOL Quarterly,* Vol. 10, No. 3 (September, 1976).

Shaw, A. M. "Foreign-language syllabus development: Some recent approaches," in *Language Teaching and Linguistics: Abstracts,* Vol. 10, No. 16. London: Cambridge University Press, 1977.

Sinclair, J. McH., and R. M. Coulthard. *Towards an Analysis of Discourse: The English Used by Teachers and Pupils.* London: Oxford University Press, 1975.

Singh, R., and J. Stanton. "Textual cohesion and sociolinguistic variation." Paper presented at the Fifth LACUS Forum, Buffalo, 1978.

Sirotnik, K. A. "Introduction to matrix sampling for the practitioner," in W. J. Popham (ed.), *Evaluation in Education: Current Applications.* Berkeley: McCutchan, 1974.

Smalley, W. A. "Review of Hendricks, 1976," in *Language Sciences,* No. 47, pp. 21-25 (October, 1977).

Smith, P. S. *A Comparison of the Cognitive and Audiolingual Approaches to Foreign Language Instruction: The Pennsylvania Foreign Language Project.* Philadelphia: Center for Curriculum Development, 1970.

Spencer, J., and M. J. Gregory. "An approach to the study of style," in J. Spencer (ed.), *Linguistics and Style.* London: Oxford University Press, 1964.

Spolsky, B. "The limits of language education," in *The Linguistic Reporter,* Vol. 13, No. 3 (Summer), pp. 1-5, 1971.

Stake, R. E. "Objectives, priorities and other judgment data," in *Review of Educational Research,* Vol. 40, No. 1, pp. 181-212, 1970.

Strevens, P. "The medium of instruction (mother tongue/second language) and the formation of scientific concepts," in *IRAL,* Vol. 9, No. 3 (August, 1971).

Stufflebeam, D. L. (ed.). *Educational Evaluation and Decision Making.* Itasca, Ill.: Peacock, 1971.

Stufflebeam, D. L. "Alternative approaches to educational evaluation: A self-study guide for educators," in W. J. Popham (ed.), Berkeley: McCutchan, 1974. *Evaluation in Education: Current Applications.*

Swales, J. *"Writing 'Writing Scientific English'," in R. Mackay and A. Mountford (eds.), English for Specific Purposes.* London: Longman, 1978.

Tash, M. *Stylistics and Language Teaching.* (Mimeographed). Montreal: TESL Centre, Concordia University, 1978.

Ure, J. "Practical registers," in *English Language Teaching,* Vol. 23, Nos. 2 and 3, 1969.

Valette, R. M. "Evaluation of learning in a second language," in B. S. Bloom et al. (eds.), *Handbook on Formative and Summative Evaluation of Student Learning.* New York: McGraw-Hill, 1971.

Valette, R. M., and R. E. Disick. *Modern Language Performance Objectives and Individualization: A Handbook.* New York: Harcourt Brace Jovanovich, 1972.

Van Ek, J. *The Threshold Level.* Strasbourg Council for Culural Cooperation of the Council of Europe, 1975.

Vaughan-James, J. C. "Report of the English section," in M. de Greve, M. Gorosch, C. G. Sandulescu, and F. van Passel (eds.), *Modern Language Teaching to Adults: Language for Special Purposes.* 2nd AIMAV Seminar with the Collaboration of ASLA (Stockholm, 27-30 April, 1972). Didier, Paris, and AIMAV, Bruxelles, 1973.

Voegelin, C. F., F. M. Voegelin, and N. W. Schutz, Jr. "The language situation in Arizona as part of the southwest culture area," in D. H. Hymes and W. E. Bittle (eds.), *Studies in Southwestern Ethnolinguistics,* pp. 405-451. The Hague: Mouton, 1967.

Wallace, W. J. "The development and assessment of an intensive English programme," in A. P. Cowie and J. B. Heaton (eds.), *English for Academic Purposes.* Reading: British Association for Applied Linguistics, 1977.

Weiss, C. H. *Evaluation Research: Methods for Assessing Program Effectiveness.* Englewood Cliffs, N.J.: Prentice-Hall, 1972.

White, R. V. "The concept of register and TESL," in *TESOL Quarterly,* Vol. 8, No. 4, pp. 401-416 (December, 1974).

Widdowson, H. G. "Directions in the teaching of discourse," in *3rd AIMAV Seminar.* Neufchatel, 1972.

Widdowson, H. G. "EST in theory and practice," in *English for Academic Study with Special Reference to Science and Technology: Problems and Perspectives.* ETIC Occasional Paper. London: The British Council, 1975a.

Widdowson, H. G. *Stylistics and the Teaching of Literature.* London: Longman, 1975b.

Widdowson, H. G. "The communicative approach and its application," in *ESP, An International Seminar,* PAIPA. Bogota: The British Council, 1977.

Wilkins, D. A. "An investigation into the linguistic and situational content of the common core in a unit/credit system," in *Systems Development in Adult Language Learning.* Strasbourg: Council of Europe, 1973.

Wilkins, D. A. *Second Language Learning and Teaching.* London: Edward Arnold, 1974.

Wilkins, D. A. *Notional Syllabuses.* London: Oxford University Press, 1976.

Williams, J. B. *Style and Grammar: A Writer's Handbook of Transformations.* New York: Dodd, Mead, 1973.

Wonnacott, R. J., and T. H. Wonnacott. *Econometrics.* New York: Wiley, 1970.

Subject Index